Understanding Human Behavior

The Complete Guide to Human Behavior, Personality Types,
and Body Language Mastery

Written By

JASON MILLER

Illustrations Copyright © 2019 by Ralph Williams

Cover photography by Ralph Williams

First Edition: December 2019

Printed in the United States of America

TABLE OF CONTENTS

PART – I The Art of Analyzing People

PART – II The Art of Manipulation

PART – III The Art of Small Talk

PART - I

The Art of Analyzing People

How to Master the Art of Analyzing and Influencing Anyone with Body Language, Covert NLP, Emotional Intelligence and Ethical Manipulation

JASON MILLER

Introduction

I had grown up at a farm where my father used to have a herd of cows and buffaloes. We also had a garden of apples that we used to sell in the market to make our ends meet. Since childhood, I knew that I was a bit different because whenever I used to meet people, I immediately formed an assessment of them like what they are thinking and how they are going to talk to me.

One day I was walking down a lonely road along with my friend Jasmine. We had just returned after plucking apples from my garden. They were not for the market but to make pickles at home. Of course, they were not ripe. It was about the afternoon when we were passing across the graveyard. Not much of a haunted place like we see in the movies where the hero along with the heroine are caught by a witch, but enough isolated to send shivers down the spine of every sensible person. When we passed through this place while coming to the garden, the sun was shining bright with full energy, but now it was later afternoon. Also, the sun was nowhere to see as the clouds that seemed to be fragile at noon were slowly covering up the sky. Now they had turned into a thick blanket that wouldn't let a single ray from the sun touch the earth.

As we paced up, a dark and gloomy person appeared to be rising over the roof of a hut that was in the graveyard. I had a hunch that something was wrong. He had not seen us until now but could have if we didn't get off the track and hid behind the bushes. Jasmine wanted to stay until he disappears, but a powerful feeling had already gripped me that we must move on while staying along with the bushes. Of course, this made some noise and movement but I was ready to take the risk. We moved on and once we were past the graveyard, we ran on the way to our home.

When we reached home, we were perspiring and our heart was pounding in our chests. The feeling of how we got away and what would have happened if we stayed there or were seen by that person, would not let me sleep at night. That night it rained like madness. Even lightning struck some trees in the jungle and they were all roasted to the ground. I waited for the morning anxiously. At last, the sun had come out and we were ready to bask in its warmth in our yard. I had taken my breakfast and now I was getting ready to go out to school. It was then that I saw Uncle Tom running toward our house. He reached in a few seconds and broke the news that a lady was murdered in the graveyard by some unknown suspect. It all happened in the late afternoon.

The news crushed me and sent chills down my spine. The horror gripped me so hard that I was unable to speak for at least ten minutes after hearing that. I knew something was wrong with that person. He was giving off such a negative human vibe that I couldn't resist thinking that he was evil personified. Anyway, my hunch and careful reading had saved me. What if he saw us? What if he catches us? Could he have done anything to us to kill evidence for covering up his crime? Could anything have happened?

At that moment I didn't know what reading of people was. I just didn't know how we got away. But I researched the subject and brushed up my skills to be perfect in reading and to analyze people.

What This Book Has to Offer?

This book contains proven methods and techniques that can equip you with the skills to read people in an efficient manner. You can learn the skills and practice them to be an expert on how to judge people. When you have mastered this skill, you will be able to guide your behavior in accordance with how the other person is ready to perceive it. In addition, you will be able to eliminate any kind of misunderstanding that gets nurtured when you misread what other person means. Let's take a look at the chapters in this book.

- The first chapter will define what the problem is with reading people. You will be able to learn how to read people and how to react to them. You will learn the skill of analyzing the head movement and studying the feet movement.

You will also get to know how you can avoid manipulation by detecting this kind of behavior earlier on in certain people.

- The second chapter will explain that people are god-gifted with the talent of reading people, but it also explains how you can learn the skill if you don't have it naturally wired in your brain. I have explained some tricks to integrate into your personality so that you can be able to kick off the learning process. Some of these tricks that you will find deeply explained are objectivity, ability to trust your gut and to find out how a person behaves naturally.

- The next chapter will explain in detail different types of people. The most prominent and discussed types include the joker, the loyal and the worker. In addition, I have explained different types of personalities like the observer, the idealist, the adventurer, and the performer. You will learn how a particular kind of person or personality behaves naturally.

- The fourth chapter hits the practical steps to reading people. You will learn how to read body language like the eyes, the hands, legs and arms. Then I will move on to the facial interpretation and analyze what facial expressions and micro-expressions to watch out for when you are reading people. You can take a notebook and write it down for reference when you are still in the learning period for reference. Then comes the turn of the inner instinct of humans and how it helps them walk safely on the road to success. The third section of the chapter will explain the importance of human vibes and how they affect our judgment of others. The human vibe can span around the eye projection, tone of our voice and the physical contact.

- The fifth chapter explains the types of liars and how you can efficiently deal with them. You will learn the techniques to protect yourself from their intentions and also help them mend their ways if possible.

- The next chapter sheds light on the adverse effects of misreading people. A flawed judgment can land our relationship in grave trouble. The chapter explains how we are prone to get confused by mixed signals and how they create misunderstandings. I have stated a number of examples about how a mixed signal can ruin our relationship. In addition, I have stated the signs to watch out for and how to react when you read a mixed signal. When you have read it, you will be better able to detect and analyze a mixed signal when you are confronted with one, and also act fast to end confusion.

- The second last chapter focuses on reading and analyzing verbal cues when you are talking to someone. It contains examples of verbal cues. Then it moves on from there to explain the difference between verbal and nonverbal cues. The chapter contains examples of a kid and a teacher and how they communicate through verbal and nonverbal signs. You can try it out on your own kids.

- The last chapter explains the importance of reading your own body language and looking into your own self. Unless you are clear about who you are and how you think, you cannot succeed in life. You will learn about the benefits of knowing yourself and concentrating on how your thinking flows. You will learn the importance of asking questions from yourself. You will learn how you can find what you like and what you dislike to make decisions faster. You will be able to know your own body's limits and how you are going to react to certain situations.

When you have read this book, you will feel yourself to be on top of every tricky situation. You will be able to judge people accurately and act accordingly. This book will equip you with proven techniques to analyze people and deal with them. This book is for businessmen, students, job-holders, spouses and almost all other categories of people. You don't need to have any special knowledge before reading this book. Anyone can buy and read this book and be a master of analyzing people.

Chapter 1

What's the Problem? – How to Analyze People Instantly Using Proven and Successful Techniques

By reading people, we don't mean that you have to read their minds like a psychic. Instead, you have to analyze their gestures and expressions to calculate what they actually mean. Reading people is about sensing their intentions like what is running in their heads through their behavior. If you gain this ability, you will be able to ameliorate your intimate and social life. When you have read and understood people, you can easily tailor your way of communication to suit their state of mind. This is how you can make an impact in a conversation.

Read People: Who They Really Are. How to Unmask Someone?

The best way to read people is not to let your emotions get over you. Forget about your past experiences. If you are trying to judge people by your past experiences, you will likely misread them. Pay detailed attention to their dressing. If they are wearing casual dresses like t-shirts and jeans, they like to be comfortable, so if they prefer comfort over hardness, they are unlikely to work hard and grow in a competitive environment. Also, see if they are wearing any pendants or stones. If they do, this indicates their spiritual inclination. This helps you judge in a better way.

Another important thing to take into consideration is a person's posture. A high head posture tells us that the person in question is highly confident. If he or she cowers, they suffer from low esteem.

In addition, the emotions that appear on a person's face tell a lot about it. Deep frown lines on a person's forehead suggest that the person is prone to overthinking. Similarly, if a person has pursed lips, he is most likely in anger and is harboring feelings of contempt. If he is grinding his teeth or has a clenched jaw, this means that he is tense.

Most people don't like to get involved in small talk. It is justified given the magnitude of our daily workload and the preoccupation associated with it. But if you ponder over it for a moment, you will realize that small talk, in fact, offers you a great opportunity to get familiarity with a stranger. You can read how he is going to behave in certain situations. That's how you are able to detect any abnormal behavior.

The Way You Treat or React to Other People Depends on the Way You Analyze Them

Once you have read people, it can greatly help you form your reaction to their questions or behavior. For example, if you have deduced that a person is highly confident and social, you will have to set your tone and posture to match his style. If he is confident but you are cowering, you two cannot have a healthy and productive conversation or collaboration.

Similarly, if a person has pursed lips, she is not in a position to listen to anything productive that you throw in her way because she is perturbed by something and will remain inattentive during a conversation. A person will only attentively listen to what you are saying if you are talking according to his or her mental state. If he is cowering and you are head high, he will feel intimidated by your posture and will not be able to open up his heart in front of you. The conversation is likely to end inconclusively or in a deadlock.

How Can You Be Accurate in Reading Someone Using Human Psychology, Body Language, and Personality Traits?

If you want to read people by means of their body language, you have to take a look at the cues that they share with each other with their gestures. Our face is one of the body parts that have considerable importance. Then comes body proxemics. This includes how your body tends to move in space. The third most important thing is body ornaments like your clothes and the jewelry you wear. Firstly, you need to decode a person's cues like interpreting the information that is hidden in their emotions and personality.

Look to Their Eyes

When it comes to reading other people's language, their eyes can be really helpful. You have to pay attention to their eye-contact and how they tend to look away while talking. If they exhibit the tendency to avoid direct eye contact, this indicates that they are not enjoying your small talk or serious discussion. In addition, this indicates disinterest and also deceit in some cases. You can also sense deceit if a person looks away or to the sides. If the person is looking down instead of looking straight, it means he is nervous. In some cases, it also shows submissiveness.

The blinking rate is also important when it comes to reading people's minds. Blinking rate increases when a person is stressed. When a person is touching his face during blinking, he might be lying to you. If the person is glancing at something, this suggests that he has a deep desire for that very thing. Similarly, glancing at a person suggests that the person desires to meet him or her or wants to talk to him or her. If he is glancing at the door, he desires to leave.

If a person, who you are talking to, is looking to the right and upwards, he might be lying to you. If he is looking to the left and upwards, he is speaking the truth. The reason is that it is natural for people to look to the left and upwards when they are using imagination. (Scott, n.d)

Study the Head Movement

The head movement of the person is also of great importance. If the other person is nodding his head when you are talking to him, it either means their patience or lack of patience. If the frequency of nodding is higher than usual, it is the indication that the person is fed up with listening to your talking and needs respite. If she is tilting her head to the sides, she is interested in your talking, but if the tilting is toward the backside, this indicates that the other person is suspicious or uncertain. (Scott, n.d)

Study the Feet

If a person is careful about his nonverbal signals, there is still one fragile point in which you can study to read what is running inside his brain. Why people miss out on controlling their feet is because they are too much focused on keeping in check their facial expressions and other verbal actions. Naturally, a person points his feet while standing or sitting toward the direction in which he wants to go. If he is pointing his feet toward you, he harbors a favorable opinion of you. If you are in a group discussion and a person whom you are talking to is pointing his feet toward some other person instead of you, this is a fair indication that he wants to talk to that person. One important thing is that feet movement and cues are meant to bypass other nonverbal cues. So, even if his facial expressions and eyes say otherwise, you have to follow the cues you pick by his feet.

How Can You Avoid Manipulation by Reading Someone's Mind?

Manipulators have one objective and that is to achieve their goals at any cost. So, their foremost weapon is using deceptive body language. There are some signs that people use when they are emotionally weak and are talking to stressors. But if this is not the case, they are very likely manipulating you by showing exactly the same signs. They will generally use these gestures to gain sympathy from you. Let's roll on to see what these gestures are and how can you avoid manipulation by reading them accurately.

They Will Rub Their Neck and Hands

When a person is manipulating you, he will rub his hands. This most likely indicates self-serving plotting. On the other hand, if he tends to rub his neck, this also signifies the same thing. The manipulator tries to gain your sympathy through this act.

They Will Stroke Their ARMS

When a person is rubbing or scratching his arms, he might have the full intention of manipulating you. This one is tricky because it is possible that the person has other reasons for scratching his arms such as hives. If scratching of arms comes in combination with neck rubbing, this may very likely be a sign of manipulation.

They Will Tap Their Feet

Manipulators tend to shift and tap their feet. This tapping and frequent shifting of feet indicate that they are impatient or even offended. Their impatience will compel you to make a decision in a rush that may most likely not be in your best interest. (English, 2019)

Chapter 2: How Many People Are Gifted with the Talent

Reading people can be a god gifted ability and you can look for certain signs that show that you have that ability wired in your brain. Upon meeting a person for the first time, you usually have a powerful gut feeling which you just cannot explain in a rational way. You instantly form an opinion whether you like them or not. And, over time, when you get to know their real self, you realize that your gut feeling was right. People cannot always explain how they were able to judge others. It is something in their sub-conscious.

Another feeling that most people have but they cannot express is the power to know other people's thoughts. This also is a natural ability. More than once you might have noticed that you were able to tell what other people had on their minds. For example, you bring up a particular topic and leave your friend wondering because he was thinking about bringing up the same topic under discussion.

Sometimes you can accurately tell if your friend is upset. You don't have to communicate with them to know that. It is just his facial expressions that you have to study in order to reach a conclusion. If you are good at this, you have this talent as a god gift.

Some people really boast of their gut feelings. They are pretty sure of escaping dangerous situations just by following their gut feeling. You might have followed your gut and saved yourself from a dangerous situation. For example, your friends are planning a trip to a lake. You cancel the plan at the nick of the time and later find out that all your friends got injured in a road accident. Have you ever had that feeling?

Some people are naturally blessed with the power to detect if someone is lying to them or not. They can tell if someone is twisting the truth or is modifying it. Perhaps they fabricate a story for their personal gains at the cost of your benefit but they don't know that you are pretty good at finding out the loopholes in their stories. Their eyes, lips and hands tell you if they are telling the truth or not.

All the above incidents are pretty common to most of us. Everyone has a particular gift to use when he is caught in a difficult situation, but most people are unable to explain its words. It remains in their subconscious throughout their lives. If you are a Sherlock Holmes fan, you can understand exactly what I want to tell you. (How To Read People Like the FBI, 2018.)

Can Anyone Learn How to Analyze People?

The ability to read people is concerned with their gestures and other nonverbal signs coupled with their words. Well, it is a fact that you can have this ability in your genes, but this is something that can be easily learned. You have to memorize different signs to accurately judge what other people have on their minds. This includes studying, memorizing and then using a person's posture, gestures, voice tone, facial expressions and also the willingness for an eye-contact in the middle of conversations. There is no rule to read people because people are different. Some have mastered the art of becoming a conman while others appear to be wearing their hearts on their sleeves. You can easily tell what they are thinking and what will be their next step? (How To Read People Like the FBI, 2018.)

Some Tricks to Learn to Read People

It is impossible that you may understand the exact thoughts of a person, but it is always possible to read how they are acting. With the help of some psychology tricks, you will be able to learn how to read people.

Objectivity

The first lesson for a learner is to be objective. You must not let your emotions and biases cloud your judgment about a person. If you have already put that person in a kind of stereotype box, you are the least likely to be right about them. Think like a neutral person.

Try to Find out the Normal Behavior of That Person

When you are trying to judge a person, you should look out for his or her normal behavior. Sometimes you miss out on correctly judging a person just because the behavior he is exhibiting is his normal behavior. This can be scratching of arms, rubbing his hands or neck, tapping the feet and looking sideways. All these gestures, we have discussed earlier, pertains to some kind of nonverbal cues, but they can be a part of a person's normal behavior. That's why you need to set a baseline for that. Calculate what is normal and what is not. Biting nails can be common with a person and cannot always be a sign of lying. If you overanalyze, you can misread people and damage your relationship with that person. Scrape this gesture and look out for some other sign that crosses the baseline that you have set for that person's behavior. (How To Read People Like the FBI, 2018.)

Are you sensing any kind of inconsistency in that person's normal behavior and body language? If you are finding inconsistency in their behavior, phoneme can greatly help you reach the right conclusion. A phoneme is a basic unit of phonetics. If the person is lying to you or feeling nervous while talking to you, she will have an inconsistent voice tone. The pith in her voice will raise or lower down while she uses particular words. She can overemphasize some words to make you believe them. At this point, you are being manipulated.

You also need to understand the context behind the speech and gestures. For example, if a person is sitting with arms crossed, it can be a sign of unhappiness. But the person's choice of taking up this posture can be due to decreasing temperature in the room. Also, you should take into account the type of furniture the person is sitting on. If the chair has no arms, then the person will naturally cross his arms to rest them. When you are in the learning phase, you should broaden your field of focus. Focusing on just one body sign will land you in confusion, and you will misjudge the other person. (How To Read People Like the FBI, 2018.)

Trust Your Gut

Last but not least is that you need to trust your gut. Pay close heed to make sense of your emotions as well as feelings. You can tell that by studying how you feel when you meet them. (How To Read People Like the FBI, 2018.)

Is It Enough to Depend on Your Instincts When Analyzing People?

Whenever we are caught up in a difficult situation, we are repeatedly told and also we tell ourselves to trust the gut. This can be a bad situation or a bad person who we think is bent on doing harm to us. The gut factor jumps in to take its toll on our nerves. But for some people, gut feeling is so powerful that they think there is no need for reading people and analyzing body language. (Chu, 2017)

A single incident, a new employee, a new boss or a new job send the wheels spinning in our heads as we try to figure out how they will impact our lives. One reason behind this immense popularity of our gut feeling is that it is a simple answer to some complex questions that keep us awake at night. Answer to all questions is: "Trust your gut."

Let me explain and clear the confusion. Our instincts are not like a magic spell. We say a phrase and things start happening or an airy creature shows itself and fills us in about a particular incident or person. Instinctual feelings or intuition are linked to our past experiences and knowledge. The reason why people have different intuitional powers is that their experiences are different. The unconscious part of our brain starts working immediately after we encounter something new. It is like pattern matching. When we see a person smiling in front of us, our brain will match this sight with loads of data that is stored in our subconscious. Then it goes on to draw a conclusion. The process is so fast that the conscious side of the brain is totally unaware of this process. That's how we receive guidance in certain situations when we feel ourselves in danger.

From this, we can deduce that if the experiences and knowledge are of greater size, our instincts work better. (Chu, 2017)

It is not enough to rely on your gut to reach a decision on whether the person is good or bad. What if you misjudge a person's intentions? When you realize his real nature, it will be too late. Take the example of a cop who, by nature of his duty, has to make fast decisions. He doesn't have enough time to scan through detailed information before he acts. So, one misjudgment can take the life of an innocent person. So, if we base our decisions only on our gut feeling, we are likely to end up making the wrong decision that could land us in trouble. The verdict is that you have to pair up gut feeling with the knowledge that you have about reading their gestures.

It is not always a good idea to follow your gut. Sometimes it is better to just eliminate the need for your gut feeling. You can do this by befriending someone and talking to them without heeding to your gut feeling. Your judgment ought to be calculated and well measured, and should be free of certain prejudices. Otherwise, you are highly likely to make a mistake and lose a friend. (Chu, 2017)

What Can You Do to Improve That Skill?

You can predict what others are thinking. You can read their minds, theorize what they are thinking and also understand their gestures. From all the data, you can know their intentions and analyze their emotions. On the basis of this knowledge, you can predict what their beliefs are and what is inside their hearts. All this makes your conversation with that person fun and productive. To achieve this feat, you should focus on brushing up your skills of reading people. Let's see how to do that.

- You need to stay focused and also be present in the current moment. Never think about yourself amid the process.
- You must be all ears to others. Listen to them attentively. Read between the lines, try to understand the context of their speech. Also, try to understand

what they are not saying and keeping back. First, process their words in your brain and try to deduce their meaning. After that, you can respond.

• While you are communicating, you ought to study his facial features, his dressing, the jewelry and makeup in case of a female. Don't forget to take a look at his or her hair cut. In addition, you should take into consideration the surroundings where you are communicating with that person. To improve your reading skills you have to be efficient when it comes to studying that person's facial features and dressing. You have to invigorate your observation skills. You should not miss out on anything minute to large. Even a slight aberration in the person's hairstyle should click your brain.

• You should not lose focus due to some intrusive thoughts. Keep it on the person in front of you. Detect any nuance in their behavior and follow how it develops.

• To improve the skill of reading people, you need to stay calm. If something is perturbing you and you are not at peace with yourself, you will not be able to read the person in front of you accurately. Inner calm is directly proportional to focus. The higher the level of your inner calm, the greater your focus will be.

• If you are the kind of person who loses patience too soon, you are least likely to read and analyze other people effectively. Sometimes you have to listen to another person's blabber on end in order to get to know them better. Practice it if you lack this ability.

Chapter 3: Different Types of People and How They Fit in the Social Circle.

All of us are full of different flaws that make us feel ashamed. We do have strengths that we want to brag about in front of everyone. Some of us prefer to stay natural in their everyday life while others love to take up their favorite persona to get through different hurdles in their lives. Some people like to make their way by deception, lies and manipulation while others prefer to face stumbling blocks but refuse to deviate from the right path. Whatever our choice of being a person in our lives is, the goal mustn't be of hiding our weaknesses as well as dark spots if we have any. We must allow our flaws to be a part of our personality. We should celebrate our flaws. This is what being human is about. When a person takes up a fake persona, he forgets that the people, who are loving him, are actually loving that persona that he has taken up and not that person who is in hiding under the fake personality. The real success is that people start loving us because of what we are and not because of what we are trying to become.

The Joker

The first category is a joker. The foremost feeling on hearing the word joker is of a person who is cracking jokes and laughing his heart out even during sober conversations. Jokers love jokes, costumes and makeup. Each makeover gives them a new look and personality. They love to hide their real looks and nature to others. Generally, jokers are considered harmless but if we bring to mind batman's joker, things get totally different. A scary and nutty person comes to mind who is evil personified. That joker is always bent on inflicting the greatest pain on the people surrounding him. Can you think of a person who fulfills the above personality traits? Do you know anyone who laughs too much, always cracks jokes or tries to tease others while laughing it out? Beware! Jokers are masters of disguise.

The Smart One

Smart people have the ability to mold themselves according to the situation. They learn or are naturally gifted to adapt to changing circumstances. Smart people always remember to read other people's styles to gain more knowledge about them. They tend to see through the motives behind their acts and also their hidden desires to work with them and gain benefits. Smart people are good at conveying their messages through in an effective manner and without making the slightest buzz. They know how to express their feelings in a clear way, which is the most important thing when it comes to building and strengthening a relationship.

Similarly, smart people are very successful in their businesses or jobs. They work hard to learn how to read people and the rest gets automatically easy for you. You can tell if a person is smart by looking at how they behave with you and other people around him. One important point to note is that smart people are very good at taking care of their personal interests, even at the cost of others.

The Worker

Workers are the people who belong to a specific social class that is known for doing jobs for low pay only to live hand to mouth in their lives. The jobs they do low demand skills and labor and also have low literacy requirements. This category of people also lives off on social welfare programs. Working-class people mostly remain preoccupied with their day-to-day expenditures. They don't have time to take up different personas and disguises. Also, they are not smart enough to get a job done in the easiest way possible. Their brains are generally wired to do it the hard way. These people generally wear their hearts on their sleeves. They are easy to predict and are simple to understand.

The Loyal

These people are hard to find but exist. They are reliable as well as truthful. If a person is loyal to you, he shares affection with you and will not leave you when life gets hard for you. Loyal people think from their hearts and always work for the benefit of the people who are close to them. Just like the working class, loyal people are easily predictable and trustworthy.

The Strong

Physically strong people generally have happy temperament. A strong person has higher levels of physical and mental strength. They don't have self-pity; that's why they are confident and good at judging people and dealing with them. Before they judge other people, they try to judge themselves. In addition, they have higher levels of self-restraint. Their nerves are powerful that's why they are patient. They also are good listeners and observers. Their physical and mental strengths make them very good at reading other people and reaching an educated judgment. They don't hesitate to ask for help when they are in need, and also, they are open to helping others.

Different Types of Personalities

People are driven by their nature when they do this or that and leave you wondering why they did something that looked unwanted to you. It is perfectly normal if you think you need to want to understand someone a bit more than you already do. This someone can be a loved one or a person at our workplace. We have to accept the reality that people are not perfect. We are different and it is this difference and diversity that makes this world a colorful and interesting place to live in. When people stay true to their role, they tend to contribute their bit to this diverse world. Just imagine if we were all created in the same way, how the world look would like then. It would be boring.

Take an example of diversity. When a car hits a motorbike in a road accident, a huge number of people gather at the site. Most of them are on-lookers who are just investigating what happened. Some mourn the wounds of the injured while some call the ambulance. Only a handful of them step up and actually help the injured recover their senses. They try to administer to the first aid and take care of them until the ambulance arrives at the site. It is not that those people leap into a house on fire without thinking about their lives. We react differently to different situations. These reactions are triggered by our fears and desires. Sometimes they motivate us while at other times, they just demotivate us.

In analyzing people, you should know the people around you. What they do and how they react to different situations. By knowing their personality types and the fears that guide their behavior, you can improve how you interact with different people. It helps you read people in a more efficient way so that your interaction with them becomes smooth and your analysis of people broadens and deepens. In addition, you can track down your own personality traits as well as faults. Let's roll on and take a look at different types of people in the world.

The Reformer / Idealist

The Reformer is a perfectionist. They have principles and are conscientious. These kinds of people have certain ideals to follow and they come down hard on themselves as well as on other people. They just love to keep them at pretty high standards. They are dedicated and responsible besides having perfect self-discipline.

They are usually successful in life because they tend to get lots of things to happen in a short span of time, and that too in the right way. They are always looking forward to setting themselves on the right path by eliminating their weaknesses. (9 Personality Types – Enneagram Numbers, n.d)

The Performer

As the title suggests, these kinds of people will always be setting goals for themselves. They are highly target-oriented individuals and they believe in doing rather than sitting on the couch and thinking day and night. They are always striving for success. This drive makes them pretty excellent at doing things right. You can find them in a big company, a shop or on the street selling vegetables or fruit. Wherever they are, their eyes are always on the horizon. They have dreams of success and they are in the world to make them happen. These kinds of people are considered as role-models by many other people.

They have their fears that drive them toward the top. What makes them perfect is their urge to become somebody. The fear of dying as nobody makes them state-conscious. Instead of discouraging others, they respect the opinion of other people. (9 Personality Types – Enneagram Numbers, n.d)

The Observer

This kind of people spend time on thinking and are of an introvert type. Their focus always is on gaining knowledge. They also prefer reading their own personality instead of reading others. They remain absorbed in themselves and love to play with different types of concepts. They usually abhor worldly attractions like big mansions, cars and social status. They are always busy in searching for themselves. They prefer to observe what is happening in their brains. You can see that these people will lock themselves in their rooms for hours as they love to understand how things go on. This exclusive behavior allows them to concentrate on what they do, that's why they are usually considered as experts on what they do. As they don't have the social skills that are needed to keep relationships healthy, they get overlooked most of the time.

The Adventurer

These kinds of people are fun-loving people. You will see them engaged in enjoyable pursuits and also, they are often in an upbeat mood. They thrive on pleasure and adventures, which makes them a really positive person. They tend to avoid negativity at all costs, which helps them fight off pessimism and stress really well. They are also very optimistic and don't let tough challenges mar their optimism. They are the ones who always find that silver lining in dark clouds. They stick to that silver lining and turn negative situations really fast and really well. (9 Personality Types – Enneagram Numbers, n.d)

Also, they are highly inconsistent. As they are fun-oriented, they remain in a certain work until the fun factor is alive but shoot out of it once they are bored no matter if the work is complete or not. Completion of projects poses a big challenge to them; that's why they struggle to be successful in the practical world.

The Warrior

As the name suggests, these kinds of people love to throw and take the gauntlet. They are strong and have dominating personalities. You can say they are born leaders and are really confident. They are real alphas. They hate to depend on other people and also don't like to reveal their weaknesses. Instead, they use their strengths to give a cover to those people who are around them as their family and friends. They are always ready to take charge of any situation no matter how thundering and dreadful it is. They love to be the masters of their own fate and they also prefer to take control of people as well as circumstances.

Their inner strength also makes them rigid, straight forward and sometimes haughty and harsh. They cannot tolerate signs of weakness in other people. They are ready to confront others on petty issues. They are always ready to express their anger and frustration on things they don't meet up with their expectations. These are the ones that are quite difficult to understand. Their nature is too intense and volatile to let others read them. (9 Personality Types – Enneagram Numbers, n.d)

Chapter 4: Basic but Proven Effective Techniques for Analyzing People

This chapter will walk you through some basic techniques for analyzing people. You will learn what body signs you have to read in order to understand what is running in the other person's mind. In addition, I will explain in detail the importance of gut feeling and the role it plays when you are trying to read other people. The chapter will also walk you through the importance of emotional energy in reading people.

I have touched upon the topic of studying body signs in the first chapter. This chapter will help you learn in detail what each body sign tells about a person.

Posture

How we carry our bodies speak volumes about our personality and mindset. The posture that we keep our bodies in tells a lot. I have earlier on explained what a straight posture indicates. I am going to add on to the previous information. When observing a person's posture, you should observe whether a person has an open posture or a closed one.

An open posture is when a person keeps the trunk of her body exposed. If you observe it in a person, she is likely to be friendly, willing and open to you. On the other hand, a closed posture is the one in which a person hides the trunk of her body. For example, she will hunch forward or keep her arms crossed. This is the opposite of openness, and the person in question will exhibit hostility and anxiety.

Body Language

Body language is the nonverbal signals that we send through our gestures. In simple words, it is about communication through our bodies. It includes our hand movements and facial expressions to as little things as our pupils. If we observe closely, we will see that people tend to give away a great volume of information through nonverbal signals. As I have already suggested, the key to reading nonverbal signs accurately is to take these signals and study them as a group.

The Eyes

Our eyes are considered as windows to our souls. They are the easiest to learn and most people can do that even without prior training. They tend to reveal a great amount of information about what is running inside our hearts. What we feel or think comes into our eyes. Even a naïve person can take the hint in the eyes of the speaker. But it is not just the eyes that should be studied. Pupils are also very important to know other person's minds. Look out for dilated pupils as they indicate increased cognitive struggle.

Pupils tend to dilate if they are looking at something they appreciate. This is not an easy job to do. If you keep observing different people, you will finally learn how to observe and detect any change in the pupils. If pupils are highly dilated than normal, it means that a person is attracted to someone and is aroused.

Hands, Legs and Arms

Gestures by hands, legs and arms are very important. I'll add on to the previously stated details. Gestures, like our eyes, carry plenty of information about our personalities. Our waving, tapping and pointing have hidden meanings that ought to be understood if you want to master the art of analyzing people. Well, it is important to sort out these gestures as some are cultural traditions like a raised straight palm. In some Asian countries, this suggests hello and in the United States, a thumbs up suggest that everything is fine. You have to keep in view these signs so that they are not mixed up with nonverbal cues.

Coming back to nonverbal cues. If a person has a clenched fist, this indicates anger but in some cases, this also indicates solidarity especially when shown by a politician or a public figure. For a clear analysis, you should study this gesture combining it with facial expressions and speech. Similarly, in some countries, people use the okay gesture that is formed by touching the index finger with the thumb. In some countries, this suggests that everything is going on fine while in parts of Europe, this means that you are nothing. In some Asian and South American countries, this gesture is considered vulgar.

Arms and legs are also quite useful in nonverbal communication. If a person tends to open his arms and keep it that way, he is an attention seeker and full of life. We have learned earlier on that crossed arms suggest closeness and defensiveness. A common gesture that you might have come across is the one in which a person stands with his or her hands on the hips. This is an indication that the person is fully in charge of circumstances and is ready to face anything. In rare cases, it may suggest aggression.

If a person clasps his hands behind the back, he is bored and anxious about something. We have learned earlier on what tapping our feet means. Besides, tapping your fingers also means a lot. It can be a sign of boredom or frustration. When a person crosses his legs, he is closing off on society and wants some personal space. He will prefer privacy than socialization.

Personal Space

More often, we are in need of personal space. Sometimes we want to mix up with people and party but sometimes we need personal space to breathe in. This happens to everyone. You might have been through the phase when you start feeling uncomfortable because of the presence of a particular person. In technical terms, this is known as proxemics. Anthropologist Edward T. Hall explains four levels of proximity between two people. Let's discuss them one by one. (Cherry, 2019)

Intimate distance: Ranging between 6 and 18 inches, this indicates that two people are enjoying a closer relationship. They are comfortable with each other. Two people come at this distance while they are hugging or touching each other.

Personal distance: Ranging between 1.5 to 4 feet, this distance suggests that two people are family members or close friends. If two people keep this distance but are comfortable in their interactions, this suggests how intimate they are in their lives.

Social distance: Ranging between 4 and 12 feet, this physical distance exists between people who have acquaintance with each other. With a coworker, the distance will shorten while with a person whom you don't know well such as a plumber, you will keep it at 10 to 12 feet.

Pubic distance: Ranging between 12 to 25 feet, this physical distance is used in public areas when you are addressing a gathering or a class or giving a presentation to your staff. (Cherry, 2019)

Apart from that, if a person comes closer to you, this suggests that he is looking for a favor from you. On the contrary, if the other person moves away, this means there is a lack of mutual connection between you two. The above-mentioned distance is not something carved in stone. It differs in different cultures.

Mannerism

Winking is a normal act between friends and intimate people, but when a stranger wink at you, it appears invasive and offensive. Wink is generally a break in eye contact which suggests that the person is trying to disrupt the flow of conversation. On a lighter note, while cracking a joke, winking is absolutely fine. Winking without reason, tends to confuse the other person. So, steady eye contact is always the way to go.

If a person has placed his arms in an unnatural position, he is not sure of himself. He is not relaxed and is suffering from a lack of confidence. The conversation with an uncomfortable person tends to be unproductive and inconclusive.

Facial Interpretation

Reading one's facial expressions is an integral part of understanding his nonverbal behavior. We have already discussed some visible expressions like winking, blinking and many other expressions. In this section, I'll briefly discuss micro-expressions. They are brief and involuntary expressions that appear on a person's face. They have great importance because it is pretty hard to fake them. Let's discuss them one by one.

A person's eyebrows will appear to be raised with a slight curve. Their skin just below the brow will appear to be stretched. His forehead will have winkles and his eyelids will remain open for a while. His jaw will appear to be dropping and teeth will be slightly parted. Their mouth will remain normal with no signs of tension.

Pay close heed to a person's lips to detect the element of disgust in their disposition. Look out for if their upper lip appears to be raised or upper teeth appear to be exposed. Also, see if his nose has wrinkles and cheeks, raised. Any such sign shows that the person is feeling disgusted.

You can detect anger from micro facial expressions. She has slightly lowered her eyebrows or drawn them together. Other signs of anger are tension in the lower lid or bulging eyes. In addition to this, if their nostrils are dilated or their lower jaw seems to be jutting out, this also shows that they are in anger.

You also can detect happiness in other people by observing their faces. She is happy if her lips appear to be drawn back. Similarly, if her mouth is parted and teeth are exposed, this is an indication of happiness. Happy people have their cheeks raised eyelids lowered with wrinkles evident underneath. Another common sign is the appearance of crow's feet on the outside of the eyes. An important thing to note is that if she is not engaging her side-eye muscles to show her happiness, her happiness is fake.

Inner Instinct

Inner instinct or gut instinct guides the physical reactions that we give to the world around us. It is the feeling that we sense when our bodies are responding to the processing of information that is stored in our subconscious, as I have briefly explained earlier on. The main purpose of our gut instinct is to give us protection in the wake of unusual circumstances. Sometimes people cannot define it but they are relying on it to deal with worldly matters. Their gut instinct guides them through thick and thin. Its power and influence vary in different people depending on their experiences and spiritual state.

Some people call it a hunch while others label it as an inkling, but in general, it is dubbed as gut instinct or instant instinct. This is different from intuition as it is our primal wisdom, while intuition is our spiritual wisdom. Both humans and animals have gut instincts. In some cases, in animals, this feeling is more powerful than humans.

Take the example of a herd of zebras. Even when they cannot see the lions that are lurking behind the bushes, they somehow sense their presence. When one of them whinnies, the rest of the herd starts racing away for cover. If you are fond of Animal Kingdom documentaries, you might have seen such scenes. Similarly, big animals like elephants rely on their gut feeling to find food and water resources.

If you are a cat lover, you can see that your cat will change its mind once or twice before it jumps over from the second story to the first story. Have you ever heard any story of hikers who got lost in the mountain trails? They had to navigate through the mountains without any compass or anything else to take help from. One of them had a hunch to go to the east and the rest of them followed him. In the end, they had successfully reached the camp. Just imagine what would have happened, had that hiker ignored his hunch.

Sometimes you have a strong feeling that something has happened to your son who is at home. You ditch the office and drive back home to find him unconscious on the floor. If you take a closer look at the world around you and also at your own life, you will find that similar incidents have been happening to you.

Signs of Gut Feeling

There are certain signs to watch out for if you want to follow your gut. The top indication is a sudden feeling of fear, especially if it is uncalled for or totally out of context. The second is a powerful urge to accomplish something just like an inner pull. You might also suffer from chills and shivers in your body. Goosebumps on your arms and body in combination with tingles up your spine also indicate that there is something wrong.

One important thing to consider is that signs of gut feeling differ for different persons. For example, some people may not experience any of the above. Instead, they get nauseous or have physical uneasiness. A few people tend to get alarmed at times while only a handful of people hear instructions or warnings in a clear voice. You might have one sign or all of them.

Discuss Intuitive Cues

Intuition means "to look within." Some scientists term it as sophisticated intelligence. People are viewing it as something that helps us make decisions rather than being a magical thing that cannot be learned. Still, the fact remains that ancient and advanced civilizations like Buddhism, Hinduism and Islam have connected intuition to the human soul. You can see if your intuition is at work by following some simple signs. You will start feeling light and clear in your mind. No emotions will affect your judgment and you will be absolutely calm and relaxed, and even inspired. If you are observing similar signs in your body and brain, your intuition is most likely at work.

Aha Moment

Things come to a standstill at times. A person who is running a clothing factory complains that despite producing the best garments in the market, customers are drying up day by day. He had run a marathon marketing plan to boost up sales but to no avail. Is more marketing the only solution? Shifting the production model can be a viable solution to the problem. Brainstorming new ideas and selling techniques is what we usually do to solve this kind of situation. But what if ideas just stop coming to us? What if nothing seems to be working? Maybe he should freeze for a moment and do nothing. Yes, this works sometimes. He should just stop pursuing a solution to the problem. Instead, he should take a shower, start playing golf or maybe watch a movie. People hit upon amazing solutions to overdue problems when they detach them from the current scenario for a while.

The key to reach the aha moment is creating an environment that is full of silence as well as solitude. These conditions are essential for your brain to nurture these moments. Ultra-quiet places are always the best for making better decisions. Once you have found a quiet place for yourself, you have to start looking inward. Focus on the live stream of thoughts. You have to detach yourself from the outer world like your cell phone and any other thing around you. When the external information ceases to reach your brain, you will slowly start noticing the aha moment. Gradually, you will achieve the "idle" mode of your brain. It is important to know that you don't have to stress out your schedule to get the aha moment. Instead, find a few quiet moments on a daily basis to do this exercise. Also, try to turn off all the electronic gadgets at least for a few hours in a day so that you can leave your brain to wonder for a while.

Human Vibe

The vibe we give off is equally important for reading people as reading their body language. This is closely linked to intuition. We run away from some people and try to be close to some of them. More often, we hear people say that they feel good or bad vibe by being around some people. Some people really elevate our mood when we are around them, while others drain us out of our positive energy.

The impact of the human vibe can be felt when we are just inches or feet away from a person. Some cultures like the Chinese dub this invisible energy as life force, named as chi. Let's take a look at a few examples.

Sometimes, your spouse says sorry to you but you feel that he is not really sorry for his mistake. A coworker is trying to charm you but you know something is fishy out there. A classmate appears to be cheerful but you have already sensed the hidden anxiety. For example, we often say that depression is faceless. People wear a smile in front of others but in reality, they are broken. While most of them around a depressed college fellow ignore her condition, you are sure that she is not healthy at all.

You need to link a person's emotions with his energy to get to know them better. Reading people by human vibe is all about decoding their emotions. By reading people's energy, you can bring yourself in line with how you relate to them, and whether you feel comfortable with them or not. If you study this subject and master it, you are able to make some crucial decisions in an effective way. For example, you will never want to spend your life as a spouse with a person who will drain your energy. The same is the case with a coworker. Why should you consume your time sharing your meals with a coworker who leaves you feeble and unproductive after a single sitting? That's why it is important that you learn how to read the human vibe.

Presence

The first thing to learn while reading people's energy is sensing the presence of people. This is the overall effect that a person leaves on you when he or she is near you. You have to calculate it. A girl in your office may leave mysterious, joyful or sad effects on you. Try to make out if the person around you is pulling you toward her. When you are reading them from their presence, try to notice if the energy they give off is warm or cold. Is it like fresh air or stalled? Do you sense anger or depression when you are near them? Whether it is a friendly sense or an intimate one when she is near you. On the basis of these readings, you can decide how to shape the future course of your relationship with that particular person.

Eye Projection

Another important method to read the human vibe is to take a closer look at that person's eyes. Eyes are the ways to transfer positive and negative energy. In Islamic civilization, eyes are considered as the source to transfer spiritual energy. Sufi poets like Rumi greatly focused on the importance of a glance. They say that the brain transmits electromagnetic signals through eyes. Looking straight into the eyes of your pet releases oxytocin which builds up a trustful and peaceful relationship between you and your pet.

You should take your time when you are observing her eyes, then study what kind of feeling you have. Is it the feeling of love, care, calm or anger? Do her eyes look sexy? Do they intimidate you? People's eyes may feel hypnotic at times. Sometimes looking deeply in their eyes make you feel insecure. That's why you have to study the effects of cautiously. If you come across a negative person, try not to engage them or they will zone in on you. If you sense positivity, keep looking straight into their eyes. Feed on all the positive energy.

Physical Contact

We share our energies with people upon touching them by means of a handshake or a hug. Whenever you touch someone through a handshake, you will know whether the person makes you feel comfortable or not. Or do you just want to withdraw? Do their hands feel clammy? This is a sign of anxiety. They will make you feel anxious. If they hold your hands in a powerful grip that your fingers feel pained, this gives off aggressive energy.

Voice Tone

Last but not least is the tone of voice in which people speak to you. It will speak volumes about their emotions and feelings. The frequency of our sounds creates distinct vibrations. Does their tone soothe you and make you calm? If you observe that the voice tone of a person is so soft that you barely hear him, this shows signs of low self-esteem. If they are too loud, this shows anxiety or insensitivity. If they are fast-talkers in your first meeting, they might want to sell something to you.

Try to observe if people are laughing too much. If this is the case, they are lighthearted. But their laugh ought to be genuine. (Orloff, 2014)

Chapter 5: Lies – Why They Affect the Way You Analyze People?

Lies go undetected more often, so do liars. Lying is quite prevalent among youngsters and this behavior hardly does any harm at that age, but when you grow older and enter professional life, liars can be harmful to your professional and intimate life. Kids consider this habit as something fun to tease their school mates and friends from the neighborhood. When they don't get caught, they consider this behavior as a way to go in life. They integrate this behavior into their personality and use it later on for personal benefits. So, that's how lying as behavior makes its way in our characters.

If you don't nip the evil in the bud, the kids will see this as a baseline for building up a powerful lying pattern to be used in the future. When you are dealing with these grown-up kids, you feel at a disadvantage because they maneuver it so professionally that you realize it only when they have already achieved their goals. It is not that liars are impossible to detect. In fact, they are pretty easy to spot around us. All we need are a few techniques to make out if a person is telling you the truth or is concealing something from you. Before we move on to analyze the techniques, we need to analyze different types of liars to make the process of detecting liars easy and smooth.

Types of Liars

Let's discuss the difference between people who are quite professional at lying. There are certain signs and symptoms that you need to watch out to find out what type of liar you are dealing with. Let's see and analyze each category to gain more insight when you are analyzing people.

Pathological Liar

The first category is the pathological liars. Pathological liars are habitual and they tell a lie in response to any kind of stimuli. They are very good at lying because of the magnitude of practice that they do. They are pretty good at fabricating stories and it is very hard to detect when they are lying and when they are telling the truth. If only you can read their facial expressions and gestures, it is easy to detect them. Look out for the movement of their eyes. If they are trying to avoid direct eye contact, they are not telling you the right thing.

If you want to understand why people lie so casually, you have to understand the circumstances they went through. They adopt pathological lying as a defense mechanism. It is a way to make their way through severe circumstances without hurting themselves. These are not excuses to become a pathological liar but these are the driving factors that push a normal person to integrate this personality trait. By understanding the pushing factors, you will be able to understand why people lie in the first place. In this way, you can stop a pathological liar midway while is weaving his web.

Sociopath

These liars are considered as the worst types of liars. They lie to achieve personal benefits without caring about how it will affect the people around them. They have a heart made of stone and they don't care about other people's emotions and even their lives. In simple words, they feed on lying. Lying is their strategy to get worldly benefits at the cost of the feelings and lives of other people. They don't feel shame or guilt at all.

When you are confronted with these kinds of people, you need to walk cautiously by carefully reading the situation. The situation can go out of control any time and you will find yourself becoming their victim in a snap. The reason is that they can turn out to be amazingly manipulative when dealing with you. They are experts in lying and they are more often quite cunning.

When you are analyzing these kinds of people, you are likely to end up reaching a wrong conclusion because of misleading or insufficient evidence. If you are currently into a relationship with a sociopath liar, you should try to free yourself of the commitment. When you are convinced that the relationship is poisonous because of the lying habit of your partner, end the relationship. You can exhaust your option of changing that person before taking a decisive step. (5 Types of Liars and How to Recognize and Deal with Each, n.d)

By now, you might be thinking that liars are like parasites who drain you of emotions and energy. But we must not forget they too are humans. They are not monsters whose only treatment is to send them in exile out in the wild or kill them with the best weapon available. It is advised that if you detect the lying habit in someone close to you for the first time, you should approach them with kindness. Show them love, tact and affection according to the size and impact of the lie that they just weaved for you or any other person. Don't forget to furnish your evidence or the other person will get away with it by denying it altogether.

It is highly likely that some liars will defend their lies and continue with it when you try to confront them, but you should keep in mind that liars have mastered the art of manipulation. Keep yourself in full senses to get away with their manipulation. (5 Types of Liars and How to Recognize and Deal with Each, n.d)

White Liars

We often see white liars around us. White lies are not real lies. At least they are not as lethal as real lies are. In most cases, they are perfectly harmless, and you can say that white liars more often tell one or the other kind of truth, that's why people believe that they are not lying. Some weak hearted people use white lies in a bid to protect themselves from the truth if they are of the opinion that truth will be damaging or hurtful for them.

When you detect white lies, you should approach those people and try to rectify their ways. If you find out that the white lie has insignificant value, perhaps you ought to let it pass. Otherwise, you can ask the liar to mend his or her ways as it is not a good idea to base a relationship on lies no matter how harmless the lies are. If you fail to detect white lies or let them pass as fun, they may cause serious problems for your intimate relationships in the long run. (5 Types of Liars and How to Recognize and Deal with Each, n.d)

Compulsive Liars

Compulsive liars are habitual when it comes to lying, but unlike pathological liars, you can detect them and figure out how to deal with them quite easily. They are not expert enough to weave a net of truth around their lies to make them appear credible to people. They are easy to analyze because they don't wear a cloak of truth over their woven web of lies. When they speak, you can tell that they are lying because they display such kind of behavior. Things to note when you meet such a person are that they will start sweating, and also they will never look into your eyes while telling a lie.

Compulsive liars can be further categorized into a habitual liar as well as a narcissistic liar. Habitual liars cannot refrain themselves from lying all the time. On the other hand, narcissistic liars make up stories about themselves. They tend to exaggerate things and like to embellish things about themselves. They will you stories how they confronted a dozen warriors and single-handedly defeated them. Other stories include how they turned out to be the hero of a number of situations like saving a girl from a raging fire. Most of the stories they tell may appear to be far-fetched. As per medical science, these kinds of people suffer from a narcissistic personality disorder. Lying becomes their habit because they feel deprived of their real lives. They have reached the conclusion that their real lives are boring and that no one is impressed with them.

How to Deal with Liars

There is a wide range of ways to deal with liars. This can be really difficult but the best approach is not to throw a fit of anger. The liar is likely to channelize your aggression toward diverting you from the subject. The best approach is to avoid getting carried away with their versions of events that you have concrete evidence of not being true. You can deal with liars by being polite and confronting them with the truth.

You have to understand the fact that all of us tell lies at one point or another. Sometimes we have to fabricate a lie to avert a crisis. Sometimes, you need to tell a lie because you don't want to hurt someone's feelings. These kinds of liars are easy to deal with because they tell a lie only to defuse a tense situation. White liars are also harmless unless they make it a habit to tell lies. What if you are confronted with a compulsive liar or a sociopath? They are habitual when it comes to telling lies.

Compulsive liars are not the easiest to deal with. In order to kill their sense of inferiority and inadequacy, they can go on to any extent to tell lies without caring for their effect on the lives of other people. They lack empathy and are unable to understand the extent of emotional turmoil that they bestow on the other people. Their dishonesty takes its toll on others. They are self-centered and can only think about their own benefit and profit.

These types of liars are the most difficult to deal with, but with greater understanding and practice, you can master the art. The first thing you should remember is to avoid confrontation with these kinds of people. They always try not to leave a trace of what they have done. When you confront them, they will come up with a new story to cover up their wrongdoing, in addition, they will become hostile in their attempt to invalidate your evidence. So, there is no point in confronting them. You have to make yourself believe that the person you are dealing with is not normal and he needs help. Think of him as a dysfunctional person who doesn't think normal. If you try to change them, they will resist any effort by hook or crook. So, you need to stop changing them. Just accept them as they are and deal with them as if they are normal. This will make them friendly toward you and it will be easier to deal with them.

The next step is to listen to what they say carefully. Don't trust it right away. It is better to retain the factor of doubt. Spare the room for verification of what they tell you. You should be careful about not letting them know what you are up to. When you are sure that the person is a compulsive liar, put a limit on the time that you spend with him; otherwise, they will keep draining you of energy and demoralize you.

These types of people don't merit your time and love. Avoid sharing your personal information and any other details with that person. Don't open up too much or they will use that information for their personal benefit. They can do that without thinking even once because of the fact that they don't have empathy for others. (Kloppers, n.d)

The next step you should take care of is that you must not expose a liar. You think that you have detected a liar and the liar also knows that. As per your impulse, you will rush toward your closest friends to tell them about that person in order to save them from his or her heinous behavior. Freeze and think for a moment. Is it really a good idea to tell others about him or her nature? The answer is a 'no.' In fact, it is pretty dangerous. The liar will behave like a suspect does on getting detected by cops. Move on in your lives as if nothing happened. Focus on what you are doing and you will be in complete comfort. In some cases, if the liar is bent on inflicting losses and pain on you, you have to do something about it. Even in these situations, think about the possible impacts of exposing them. Better have a comprehensive discussion on the subject with the people who are close to you.

When you have decided to expose a liar, you should do this carefully so that you don't paint him or her in a negative picture. Try to convince others that he or she did that out of sheer necessity. This will paint your picture positively in the eyes of the liar. That's how you can expose him and also succeed in gaining his sympathy. In fact, this can promote friendship between you two.

In severe circumstances in which the chances of confrontation are high and moving on also is not a good choice, the only way is to show that you understand why the liar committed that wrong act. Not only show them by gestures or expressions but also try to tell them in clear words that you understand why they did that. Tell that it is normal to do that for self-protection, and also tell them that you accept them. That's how we are actually telling them that what they did was wrong but we are forgiving them. This has the potential to change their hearts. Perhaps they decide to mend their ways.

The above method doesn't always work. Some people tell harmful lies without shame or regret. They even inflict serious losses on people by telling lies. They are the ones who ought to be exposed so that other people should be saved from their lethal actions. You must not fear of exposing them and getting into a direct confrontation. They have already inflicted losses on so many people that there will be hardly anyone left who will show sympathy toward them. The people whom he has done wrong will support you. When we are done exposing them, we should immediately part our ways with them and become more cautious.

Compulsive liars are without a doubt hard to deal with. There is no hard and fast rule for the purpose. You have to read the person and then tailor your reaction to suit the circumstances. Without much homework, you will only land in trouble.

Chapter 6: Adverse Effects of Misreading People

This chapter is going to walk you through the effects of mixed signals. You will learn how people misread each other's signals and how it lands them in trouble or at least create a web of confusion among them. Reading people, though seems easy, is a tough nut to crack. If you miss out on a key signal and misinterpret it, you are going to misread someone's intentions. Bad intentions will be interpreted as good while good as bad. Similarly, wrong judgment will hamper our social connections or relationship with our colleagues.

This suggests that you should know the consequences of misreading people so that you may remain cautious. One wrong decision may land you in trouble. Mixed signals are dangerous in the sense that they confuse you, and confusion edges you off the right track. You should know what mixed signals are and how you can deal with them to avoid a crisis situation. This chapter also carries examples of mixed signals and the ways to tackle them wisely.

Mixed Signals

I have a friend named John who got a job at a grocery store. There he had a team of around a dozen people. As a good manager, he used to call a meeting every Thursday. Each meeting had an agenda that John followed in letter and spirit. John tells me that he wanted to be as handy to his staff as was possible. He used to help them in packing and putting groceries on the shelves for display.

John believed that he couldn't do more for the staff. Unlike most other bosses, John was a really good listener. He always welcomed criticism, suggestions and new ideas to improve the look of the store and boost sales. He was pretty satisfied with his role in the store. One day he welcomed criticism on his own performance in the store, so he requested his staff to criticize his shortcomings. Literally no one appeared at the meeting, suggesting that they had no issues with his style of running the store. After insisting for a week, one employee appeared in his office and opened up his heart. He said, "Mr. John, why do we think that we cannot do our jobs right. Why do you always come up to give us a hand? Don't you have confidence in our abilities?" This was completely shocking for John. He didn't think that his offer to help his staff would be perceived in another way.

John thought that by helping her staff, he would be able to identify with them. They will feel relaxed and satisfied, but the result was completely different from what he had thought. Instead of considering John a generous and kind person, his team felt a kind of inferiority complex.

This kind of scenario may happen and we don't even know about it. John's staff misunderstood his intentions. They perceived it as a lack of faith in their ability to do the job efficiently. These misunderstandings herald conflict as well as resentment, and this kind of misunderstanding is pretty common between couples. This story is also related to John. Compelled by his kind and affectionate nature, John wanted to hire a maid for her wife who was pregnant, and he did that accordingly. On the contrary, his wife thought that John didn't like the food she used to cook for the family just because he had passed critical comments on one or two dishes she had cooked. Despite the fact that you have explained that you are hiring the maid to relieve your wife of workload, but the seed of misunderstanding has already been sown.

Take a critical look at your own married life. There might be more than one occasion when you and your wife misunderstand each other for insignificant reasons. For example, you might be dining while your wife is telling a story to you. Although you are all ears to your wife yet she might find the act of your dining while she is speaking offensive. This may lead to a potential misunderstanding between you two. Similarly, you two have made a plan to go to a beach for sunbathing. Your wife feels sick and excuses herself from going with you. Although her excuse is genuine yet you might think that she doesn't want to go with you. Similar incidents of misunderstanding may happen when you two disagree on simple things like watching a movie together.

So, there is usually a big gap between what we say and how our listeners perceive it. The difference between real meanings and perceptions is not always a matter of egocentrism. Mixed signals are complex to understand but they have great importance when it comes to reading people. Mixed signals confuse you and land you in a blind spot where you cannot think clearly or see things how they are in reality. These signals cloud one's judgment of people and circumstances.

Take the example of a dating scene. You are dating someone who is not responding to your texts, but after some time, she reads your Whatsapp status or Facebook story. You will be confused. The point to understand is that we, as humans, lack perfection when it comes to expressing our thoughts. This is also true that we improve on our experiences and try to streamline our understanding of others' thoughts. Still, our true feelings tend to get hidden in how we translate them into actions and how we communicate through our speech. So, we can say that mixed signals are negative signals because that's how we are going to perceive them. One in hundred, if not thousands, will see something good in a mixed-signal.

So, should it go that way? Is it destined to be that way? There is an antidote to this problem. When you are confused about the inner feelings of a person, you should read their words coupled with their actions. But this demands practice, a lot of it, to decipher that hidden meaning accurately and perfectly.

Why Do People Give off Mixed Signals?

If you are receiving mixed signals, all burden is not upon you for reading her accurately. She also has to streamline lots of things. Mixed signals lead to miscommunication in most cases, and this affects the health of your relationship. Sometimes people intentionally use them to keep someone at arm's length because they just don't want to engage with them. For example, your fiancé is fed up with the relationship, but she cannot express it in words as it would be hard to hear and also, it would lead to an endless debate which she definitely wants to avoid. Here, she will start sending mixed signals to you. Like ignoring your texts but talking to you on phone or ignoring your call and responding to your texts, so that you take the hint that she doesn't want to be with you anymore. That's why first she will slow down the pace of the relationship and then she will say goodbye so that everything concludes making the least possible noise.

The story doesn't end here. Mixed signals don't always mean that the other person is trying to avoid you. It also is a way to cope with the stress that comes from getting intimated and close to other people. Your girlfriend might be going through this phase of stress, and you unknowingly end the relationship blaming her for intentionally avoiding you. Let's take a look at some mixed signals that sabotage relationships.

They Don't Meet up Your Expectations

There might come a moment in your life when you keep waiting on end for a special person in your life to respond to your texts or Whatsapp status. It is normal behavior to send and text and then expects a response to it right away. Absence of which can cause confusion and misunderstanding, and may mar your relationship in the long run. It is normal that the other person might be caught up in work. You will wait for the first few minutes but when a considerable length of time has passed, frustration will come to hit you hard. You will start feeling off about it.

It is possible that they will respond to you when they are free and when they find it convenient. In order to have a clear view of the circumstances, you should note if this kind of behavior has become a habit with them or not. One thing is clear from a recurrent behavior that the person is not fully dedicated to you.

Half-hearted Effort to Meet You

"I am dying to meet you. When will we meet? I am planning to drop in this weekend. Stay free." She texts you thrice a week but has not yet found time to come over on weekends and spend time with you. Every time she misses a weekend, she texts you saying that she remained busy. One or the other assignments keep her from coming over to you. She says that she has to juggle responsibilities and priorities. You remind her that she is placing other things as top priorities and ignoring you. People are not busy at all. It is all about priorities. When she has decided to meet you, she will find a way out. If she is not doing that, she has other things at top priorities. That's why she is unable to fulfill her commitment to you. Maybe she is sending you a mixed signal for a reason. Take the catch and make a decision.

She Doesn't Open up as She Should Be

When a relationship kicks off, you expect your partner to share everything with you like the names of her friends, information about her exes and lots of other things. It is this transparency that helps in cementing the foundation of your relationship. When the two of you have shared everything with each other, you will be able to form an emotional connection, which sets things off. Both you and your partner need to share their bit for a healthy connection. If you are sharing everything while she seems to be holding back, this is not a good omen for the relationship. The foundation will have cracks right from the start, which will eventually bring down the entire structure one day. Therefore, if you sense such a behavior, take it as a deliberately mixed signal. Analyze it and make a timely decision instead of delaying and regretting afterward.

Does Your Partner Flirt with Other People?

This turns out to be painful than other signals for lots of people, but this is also an important one to study if you want to make accurate assessments. This happens in thriller movies. The hero has a girlfriend who is a bit friendlier with his friends. At first, everything seems to be normal but slowly, you realize that she is up to something else. Do you remember a scene from any Hollywood movie in which hero plans for camping beside a lake along with his girlfriend and college fellows? At the campsite, she pays more attention to the friends of the hero. The hero gets confused at first due to the mixed signal. Then gradually, he realizes that something is fishy. His girlfriend is not actually interested in him. She is keeping all options open so that if one doesn't work out well, she could jump to the other.

The solution is not to frame allegations around her but keep patience. Ponder over how she is dealing with your friends. Note the dialogues, the gestures and the frequency of their meetings in addition to the time she spends with them. When you are sure that something is wrong, you should take her out for a walk at someplace where your friends couldn't reach to disturb you. Now you ask her in clear words about what is happening and why is it happening? You can request her to change her behavior because the current behavior unsettles you. If she truly cares for you, she will try to tone down her behavior and keep herself in check. If she doesn't try at all, take this mixed signal as a clear sign to make a decision. It is better to part ways than regret afterward.

She Cares for You When You Are Alone but Doesn't Show Affection When You Two Are in Public

Watch out for this mixed-signal carefully. She is ready to make out with you while you are at home. She is super comfortable while talking to you on end and watching a movie with you, but when you are out with friends for a hangout, she is unwilling to be seen with you. She just doesn't want to open up about her relationship with you. If your relationship is in its infancy, you should give your partner some time to adjust herself in your and her friend circles. When she is comfortable enough, the relationship will take a smooth road and move on well, but if she continues to behave like that after a while, you should take this signal with caution. Perhaps she made a hasty decision and now she is regretting. She may be pointing toward the underlying tension that exists in your relationship. Maybe she doesn't want to be seen with you anymore in public but is too polite to tell you so.

Remember that when a person truly loves you, their words and actions go on well. If she promises you to show up at your office when your boss throws a party for you and she doesn't keep it, these signals should be taken as serious. Like all other mixed signals, you have to give her some time. After three to four incidents, you will be better positioned to make a decision.

Chapter 7: Analyzing Verbal Cues

In order to know the difference between the truth and deception, you have to follow certain cues. The signs of lying are not clear; hence they are hard to understand. In addition, you cannot always be sure whether a person is lying or not. By practice, you can be able to tell if someone is lying to you or not easily. The rule is simple. When we are lying, we are deviating from how we behave naturally. We have to make an effort to look truthful while we are lying; that's why if you know how a person behaves naturally, you can easily tell when they are lying by tracing the difference in their behavior. The difference can be the inclusion of certain words or phrases that he normally doesn't use.

Look for Deviations in Their Words

Inconsistencies can help you distinguish the truth from the lie. For example, a person at your office tries to convince you that he didn't meddle in your documents. If he is telling the truth, he will not care what you like to listen to from him. Otherwise, he will formulate a plan in his brain. He will brainstorm what words and phrases should be used so that he may look truthful before you. The phrases like, "I didn't do that. I wasn't in the office at that time. How could if do it?" should be enough to put him under suspicion. In addition, he will repeat these words and phrases again and again. Experts believe that this kind of repetition buys them more time to think and fabricate another phrase that could convince you that he didn't do it.

Another verbal cue is that he will tell you more than you need to listen. Chances are high that he is telling you a lie. Liars talk too much because they have made it a habit to fabricate lies. They're uncalled for openness should be enough to alarm you.

Another indication of a liar is that they find it pretty hard to speak when you try to ask questions from them. They will stammer, lose words and find them entirely speechless. The reason for this kind of behavior is psychological. Their mind is not ready for rapid questions. Liars make up stories when you ask them a question. After one or two questions, they find them at a loss. Another reason is that our automatic nervous system malfunctions during stressful times. This dries them out of answers, which is an indication that they are telling lies. Also, watch out if they are biting or pursing their lips or not. Any such behavior is an indication of a liar.

Learn to Ask Right Questions

Parents have to believe what their kids say to them. When they say they were with their best friends whom you know very well, you believe them without investigating the truth. But when they tell the same thing again and again, this means there is something fishy in the bottom of the story. Teenagers want to do lots of things that pass their mind and to make it possible, they tend to tell lies to their parents so that you their parents or teachers approve of their activities. When they suspect that a particular activity would not be approved, they tell outright lies. This is the time to worry.

If you level allegation of lying against them, they will become hostile to you right away, and this will only make them more stubborn. That's why you need to be tactful to make them realize that their lie is not working without them knowing that you are manipulating them. That's where you need to use the technique of Volatile Conundrum. Try to create a scene. Ask your son the right question. Ask him where he went with Jimmy, the name he used to deceive you. Jimmy is his classmate whom you approve of if your son remains with him.

"You got home pretty late at night."

"Where did you go with Jimmy?"

He would say that they were at McDonald's to celebrate the birthday of their friend from school.

Here you have to come up with your own version of the story. "Really? I heard that a minute fire broke out at McDonald's due to short-circuiting. Did everything go well? When did the fire brigade reach the site?"

Now, this is the momentum where your son will be caught in a conflict. Whether to approve your version of the story or deny it altogether? If he approves of it right away in a snap decision, you have successfully caught a liar without confronting him. If he disputes the fact that the fire didn't break out but in reality it did, again you have successfully caught a liar. In this way, you have successfully put your kid in a Volatile Conundrum situation.

Knowing How and When to Read Verbal Cues

All of us use verbal cues almost every day. Have you ever wondered how do you communicate with people? What are the ways in which you communicate with them? Communication is not a simple process that you can easily understand. It is rather a complicated process that is so detailed that you cannot miss out on a single nuance without miscommunicating what you have on your brain. There are little things that you take into account during communication such as your reaction when someone tells you a joke. Whether you should laugh, smile, or don't do anything at all. We usually get ready to laugh when we are sure that the person has delivered her punch line of the joke. Some laughs are spontaneous. You just cannot wait to understand before you laugh whether it is the punch line on which you are laughing or not. So, that's complicated. What if you laugh before the punch line, would it not sound awkward? What if you have delayed the laugh? Now the other person will be in an awkward situation.

You have to look for verbal cues when you are communicating with someone. In communication, cues are generally considered as prompts that you can use to show others that it is time for them to issue a response or give a reaction. A verbal cue can be a word, a pause in language, rise in the tone or fall in it, or anything else related to speech. For example, I asked my friend, "Shall we try our luck in starting a new business for the two of us?" Now I have put up a question for my friend and I expect a response from him. There should be an answer or the communication will hit a stumbling block.

Verbal cues are more important when we have to teach children at home or at school. Children are not so accustomed to understanding non-verbal gestures like facial expressions and body language. You have to explain everything in words before them. When a teacher has taught kids a lesson on the whiteboard. She asks them, "Can anyone draw a circle on her page like the one that is drawn on the whiteboard?" She will for sure use nonverbal gestures like pointing her hands toward the circle and toward the pages that are put in front of them on the desks. So, that's how with the help of clear words teachers are able to communicate their questions and instructions to the students.

Take another example. The teacher has taught the kids about circles and the way to draw them. They come the next day to the class. The teacher plans to take a surprise test about circles. She will draft a question in her head that will be easier for the kids to grasp and respond to. Perhaps she says to them, "You remember what we learned yesterday?" At least a few of them will respond in the affirmation. Now she says, "Who will come up and draw a circle on the whiteboard?" This is the question that the kids will understand and respond to you accordingly.

Direct and Indirect Verbal Cues

You need to know the words when communicating with other people. Direct verbal cues are clear statements or instructions. Parents are quite skillful in these verbal cues because they have to raise kids. Even new parents find out ways to train the children because verbal cues are integrated into our nature. Let's see some example of verbal cues that a child understands easily and integrate into his or her brain to use it in the future.

- Come to me.

- Go and clean your bedroom.

- What are you chewing?

- What are you studying?

- Why have you come so late from school?

- What are you thinking about?

- Have you brushed your teeth?

- Did you put the blender on the rack?

- Where are your books?

- How did your exam go last week?

So, these are the questions that we ask our kids every day. These examples contain clear instructions for the kids that's why they understand them right away and respond accordingly.

The second type of cues is indirect verbal cues. These also are considered as prompts but they are quite less obvious than the direct cues. I mean they are just not direct questions with a clear question mark at the end. When a teacher shows up in the class and puts the following questions?

- Has anyone seen my pen?

- Has anyone got an electric clock?

- Have you understood the concept well?

- Does anyone know how to draw a circle?

- Will anyone show up at the desk to draw a circle?

These questions are not specific to a single student. Instead, these are general questions. Only the students who will relate to them will respond to them accordingly. In simple words, we can say that indirect verbal cues throw the ball in the court of the listener. It is him or her who will decide whether to respond or not, how to respond and when to respond. The prompt in indirect verbal cues are not directed to any specific person. See the following examples:

- What are you going to eat today?
- What have you done from dusk till dawn today?
- What work have you done to clean the house?
- How did you bake the cake?
- How are you going to get a job in NYC?
- What are you going to do in the evening?

Chapter 8: Looking into One's Own Self

It is a proven fact that magic crystals, tarot cards, palmistry and astrology can help develop your psychic skills but still, the most direct and effective method to know about yourself is to connect with your own mind. If you really want to connect with your own self, you will have to invest considerable time in reading your habits and how you behave. Just like meditation, you have to stay away from television, radio, and mobile any other activity that would engage you to mind. There should be no children or pets around you while you are on your way to finding yourself. You can turn on light music if it helps collect your thoughts but you can also sit in complete silence if it makes you comfortable. Let's take a look at some key benefits of self-knowledge.

Benefits of Self-Knowledge

There are certain benefits that you need to take a look at in order to be motivated for exploring yourself.

- Knowing yourself will offer you a special kind of pleasure and happiness. You are in a position to tell other people who are. Your expression is confident and smooth. When you know what you desire for, you can express it in simple words.

- Knowing yourself helps you improve your decision-making. When you tend to know yourself, you are better able to make certain choices about the world. These can span from making small decisions to big ones like choosing your partner. You are more ready to tackle the problems of your life and also find solutions for them.

- Knowing yourself offers you self-control. The ability to know yourself helps you understand what motivates you to put a stopper to bad habits and what is needed to adopt good habits.

- Good knowledge of your own self helps you resist social pressures that are constantly mounting upon you from one or the other sides. When you know what you like and dislike, you are more ready to say yes and no to certain people and their proposals.

- This also makes you more willing to tolerate and understand other people. You are in a good position to know your own struggles which helps you identify with other people. This instills more tolerance in your personality. (Selig, 2016)

Let's see how you can know yourself.

Concentrate on Yourself

Before you go on to knowing yourself, you should clear your mind first of any intrusive or lingering thoughts that come to obstruct your mind. Bring yourself in a position in which you are the least distracted. Just focus on the current moment. You can try to focus on an imaginary point in your brain. Stabilize that point and try to find a grounding place where you find harmony. You need to focus on that point until your brain is free of negative thoughts. Concentrate on the white light of your consciousness. Feel the calm this state has brought to you. When you are no more distracted by negative thoughts, you can move on to the next step.

Ask Questions

Throw questions before your psychic self. This is where you can start thinking about your life and get answers from your own self. Before going into this procedure, you need to have a clear idea of what you have been trying to find out about you. It is always a better idea to jot down these questions on a piece of paper and memorize them. Now ask them from yourself. See the following examples:

- What is the perfect job for you?

- Where do you want to live?
- What type of partner do you want to have for you?

Try to be as clear as possible in asking questions. Vague questions will only produce muddled answers.

If you are doing it for the first time, it will be hard to get answers in the first go, so if your brain is empty of answers, don't take it to heart. Instead, keep trying to explore yourself. Give yourself time and space to settle on what you are trying to ask it. Keep your body and emotions in a fair check. You might feel unexplained sensations in your body or some emotional reaction. Don't ignore them. Note them down and try to see what they are trying to explain.

Gradually, you will be able to find the much-needed answers to your questions. Persistence and the right practice are keys to it. If you start curbing your emotions, you are binding your brain which is not good. Let every emotion and feeling flow naturally so that they may aid you in finding the right answers.

Know Your Personality

You should have complete knowledge of your personality. You think that you know yourself because you know who you want to meet, what you like in food and what you dislike, how you want your partner to be and behave. But have you ever experienced a situation in which you couldn't explain how you reacted in a certain way? We deal with certain people and things which we regret later on and even feel ashamed of. Still, we cannot explain why we reacted that way. How do you react to failure, success, a challenge or a bad day? All these things matter much.

Find out Your Core Values

Your core values, moral codes, and principles always remain dear and near to your heart. There are certain values on which you just cannot compromise. These values will ultimately affect your decision-making ability, the power to resolve conflicts, your way of communication and your day-to-day living style. Find out what they are by deep introspection, as I stated in details at the start of the chapter. Are they honesty, flexibility, integrity or security? Are you soft-hearted, dedicated to the cause of others, prone to learning, wise or a leader? Once you have agreed on what your core values, you be more than ready to analyze other people and also mend your own ways when you stray away from the right path. (be your own psychic – 5 steps to give yourself a psychic reading, n.d)

Know Your Body

Our body is as complex as our brain is. Whenever you start to know it, it changes. When we are children, it is pretty different than when we get old. It remains a piece of a mystery until death because we don't take an interest in exploring its limits. It is full of surprises. Sometimes these surprises are positive while at other times, they are absolutely shocking. Did you ever think what your breathing pattern is? What are your abilities? How flexible are you? How much balance can you bring in your walking pattern? (be your own psychic – 5 steps to give yourself a psychic reading, n.d)

There are times when we say no because our body has reached a certain limit. I cannot do this or I cannot do that. Our body feels challenged. Here you need to take the time to become intimate with your own body such as your strengths and weaknesses. Whether you are comfortable in cold weather or hot weather or balmy weather are things that you must know about you. Many people claim that they know themselves but in reality, they are missing out on clarity. They are just not clear about their mind and vision. (be your own psychic – 5 steps to give yourself a psychic reading, n.d)

You Need to Know Your Dreams

All of us have dreams of a great work future, kids and a luxurious lifestyle. We dream about so many things that we get confused which is the thing that we want more. What are our preferences? Knowing dreams are important and they are worth going after. Get to know them and prioritize them in your brain so that when someone asks you, you are able to speak about them clearly without stammering or repeating.

If you are confused about a dream, ask yourself if you want to do a certain thing. For example, you want to become an interior designer. Gather all the details about this profession. Now ask yourself if you can accept this profession with all its intricacies and liabilities. If you find the answer in affirmative, you need to integrate your dream in your daily pursuit of goals. If you find out that the dream existed in your mind without any reason and that you are not sure whether to pursue it or not, just discard it and never let it distract you in the future. (be your own psychic – 5 steps to give yourself a psychic reading, n.d)

Know What You Like

We believe that we know what we like but in reality this is not true. When someone knows himself, he is highly confident when dealing with others and doing some kind of work. The confidence is evident in his acts and speech. Almost every one of us gets carried away with the popularity of things thinking that we like them but the feeling wears away with time, leaving you confused.

Knowing yourself means that you know your likes and dislikes up to the extent that you are able to write them down on a piece of paper without thinking much when you are asked to do that. Ask yourself the following questions. (be your own psychic – 5 steps to give yourself a psychic reading, n.d)

- What are the foods that you like the most?

- Who are the people you like to meet more often or who give you a pleasurable feeling?
  - Which fruits do you love to eat?
  - Which vegetables are your favorite?
  - Which family members make you feel comfortable when they come to meet you?
  - Which friends are annoying to meet?
  - Do you like mobile games?
  - What type of clothes do you want to wear?

You need to start learning by looking into the mirror. Sort out what you like and what you don't. Now all you have to do is to stay true to your likes or dislikes. If you keep doing what you don't like and also ignore what brings you joy, you are doing great injustice to yourself. In fact, you have become ready to give up your own personality. In simple words, you are not going to be happy. On the other, hand, if you take care of your likes and dislikes, you are more likely to be happy. (be your own psychic – 5 steps to give yourself a psychic reading, n.d)

Practice makes you perfect. The more you practice, the better you will get on reading people. When you know yourself, you are better able to see others in a clear

Conclusion

Social cognition means how we understand people. This enables us to predict how they will behave and how they will share certain experiences. In addition, it is also critical that we understand certain nuances in everyday speech to make out the hidden verbal cues in the speeches of our colleagues and bosses. Many a time people don't mean what they say and don't say what they actually mean. For example, when someone says, "it is getting cold." It indirectly means that you should go and close the window or the door. You can easily understand the hidden meaning in the remark.

Practice makes us understand what is running in the minds of people, even if they don't speak it out. This is how we can understand their beliefs, experiences and feelings. When we place ourselves in others' shoes, we tend to learn how they think and will behave in a certain situation. This is the start of our understanding of our colleagues and family members.

Reading people is complex. Have you ever had a look at a person and figured out how that person thought or what his nature was? Did you reach the right conclusion? Or did you make a mistake right from the start? The conclusion doesn't matter. What matters is that you tried to make a judgment. If you are always right about your judgment, you are a lucky person because there are so many people in the world who have to go through lots of reading and practice sessions to be able to read other people perfectly. You always need this skill, whether you are an executive in a company who has to run a team of a hundred people or an employee who has to do lots of work and keep his boss happy. The need for reading people increases when you change a job or meet a new boss. Only after a careful judgment of that person, you are able to better communicate with them.

Similarly, at home, you have to read the mood of your father and mother, especially when you have to communicate something important such as your marriage proposal, some girl or boy you like or about the future of work. Only when they are in a good mood, you can be able to say and be heard positively what you want to say. Perhaps you have scratched their favorite car so you will have to catch them in the right mood to communicate that tragic news to them. If you misread them, you will land yourself in great trouble.

Reading people is important and there is more than one reason for that to prove that this is a good skill to add to your skillset. Now that you have gone through the book, you can understand that reading people is essential before you approach a person to talk to him or her. If that person looks friendly, you can go on and open your heart to him; otherwise, you may decide to hold your feelings a bit longer. This skill can enable you to judge if your friend is upset. You can go on to know the reason of his disturbance and help him accordingly. If you are a master of reading and analyzing people, you are very well on the road to success at your workplace. You have to meet people who have different types of behavior. If you misjudge a cunning person and tell him your secrets, you have brought doom to your life by your hands. Similarly, if you have misjudged a sincere person and kept him at bay, you are missing out on a pure friendship that could have helped you climb the ladder at your workplace.

In addition, if you have to gain expertise in the skill of reading people, you are well on your way to be a social magnet. You can easily read people and judge the situation and tailor your communication accordingly. That's how you can win lots of friends and get popular in your social circles. For example, if people appear to be friendlier, you can approach them with a smile on your face and informal greetings. Otherwise, you can take up a formal persona and deal with them accordingly. So, reading people helps you take up a fluid personality that you can shape up according to the expectations of those around you.

This is a general rule. When you say things that others want to hear or behave as others expect you to do, you become a popular figure in your circles because you have mastered the art of keeping them in comfort zones those near you. Your social circles will remain full to the brim always. Understanding the feelings of others is an art that helps you anticipate what is running in their minds, which can help you tailor your speech.

The world is full of confusion. Misreading people leads to a flawed judgment that in turn leads to an inaccurate assessment. Sometimes, a misread facial expression can lead to cracks in the relationship and cause the death of it. For example, she loves you but just doesn't want to talk to you because she had a bad day at work, but you misread her facial expression and distance yourself from her. No matter how nicely she explains her position to you until you read it yourself, the element of doubt will remain in your mind. This small element can plague the entire relationship in the days to come.

So, reading people plays a crucial role in shaping up your intimate relationship. In addition, it can help you at your workplace. This book has walked you through the methods you can use to read people. These methods include reading people with the help of understanding their body language like the movement of their hands and arms, how they sit or how they walk. I have also explained in the book how you can read the facial expressions of a person to judge what he is thinking or what he has to say to you. You can read people by some pretty micro facial expressions to better your judgment of them.

A chapter in the book explained different types of people and different personalities that people take up to move through this life so that you have a better know-how of which type of personalities exist and what is the mindset that is linked to each personality. This will help you better judge people when you are able to identify them with a personality that you have read and integrated into your brain; the process of reading them gets smooth and easy. You also learned about the gut feeling and how it plays a crucial role in guiding your decision-making in day-to-day activities. In addition, you learned about the human vibe and how it can be linked to reading people. How you can study emotional energy and know how the other person makes you feel when he is close to you and how is he going to deal with you and whether you should keep in contact with him or not for the long term.

The book also explained different types of liars like what are their types and how they are you can deal with them. What steps you should avoid and what steps you must take to tackle them. You have learned the adverse effects of mixed signals if you misread them. Mixed signals have ruined lots of relationships and it continues to do so, just because we lack skills in sorting them out, and we always make a hasty decision.

I hope you have learned a lot and have started sorting out things in your brain. We have the basics of reading people in our subconscious. All we need is to sort it out by studying what a typical reaction means and then start implementing it on our social interactions.

PART - II

The Art Of Manipulation

Master the Art of Manipulating and Influencing Human Behavior with Persuasion, NLP, and Dark Psychology

Jason Miller

Introduction

When I was at school, I always wanted to be a public speaker. I didn't know that how difficult it was to be one or how challenging it can be to maintain the reputation of being a public speaker. Still, I went on with the venture and trained to speak in the public. I started with college functions and then went on to take part in debate competitions. I loved the feeling that the hall full of people was attentive to what I was saying to them. It was an amazing experience.

I often wondered how some people wielded magical influence over the rest of the lot. How a bunch of people managed to stay at the top all the time. I idealized the personalities of Martin Luther King and other revolutionaries who enjoyed massive public appeal. When they spoke, people listened to them. What they said to them, they remembered it. What they asked them to do, they abided by. Martin Luther King is no more but still his speech keeps ringing in my ears. I feel inspired and influenced. I want to make it happen what he said in the speech. I want to follow him. Just look at the power of the influence he had exercised and still exercises over the masses.

Incredible is the only word we can give it. These people were inspirations. They used to be massive crowd pullers. The thought crossed my mind more than once how could they manage to make people act on their words? Their power over the masses was just unbelievable. What methods they used? What were the words they chose to speak when they were making calls of action? How they used to dress? What were the books they liked to read? What was their talking style and what gestures were common to them when they talked to a single person and what gestures they made when they used to address a massive crowd? All these questions made a chain and kept spinning in my head while I grew older. In this book, I have taken the liberty to answer all those questions. I want you to know what techniques you can adopt to make yourself a highly influential person. How you can make people to like you? How can you be their leader?

What This Book Has to Offer?

This book carries methods and techniques to make yourself a highly influential person. You can read it, integrate the techniques into your personality and exercise a magnetic influence over the masses. Let's breakdown the chapters of the book and see what they have got for you.

- The first chapter of the book revolves around the topic of manipulation. It carries details on manipulation in a relationship and also the existence of covert emotional manipulation in intimate relations. You will get to learn an in-depth analysis of different manipulation techniques that are used by people. Some of the top techniques are devaluation, gaslighting, lying, projections, targeting victims and playing the victim card. When you move on into the depths of the chapter, you will get to know how you can deal with emotional manipulators. Then you will learn about the techniques to spot a manipulator in your friend circle and in intimate relationships. The chapter also carries details on the early warning signs of psychological manipulation. The chapter ends in telling you how you can handle manipulation like a pro.

- The second chapter of the book focuses on persuasion. You will learn the importance of a good first impression that includes being punctual, being original and also the importance of small talk. The chapter also carries details on how to build your rapport with people. How you can communicate in a better way and how you will be able to set expectations. You will learn how you can be able to persuade people with the help of emotions and pain. Other topics in the chapter include the elements behind motivation of human beings. The chapter ends up in explaining how you can answer questions with the help of questions to ease out the pressure accumulated on your nerves, and also certain softening statements that you can learn to make a perfect impression the people around you. The chapter contains the perfect recipe for being able to persuade the people around you.

• The third chapter spans around the methods that can help you learn how to influence people. This chapter is one of the most important chapters of the book. On the back of the knowledge that you have gained in the first two chapters, this chapter goes on to explain different techniques such as brainwashing technique, the features that matter in influencing others, the principle of reciprocity, the pre-giving technique, the foot-in-the-door technique, low-balling offer, the that's not all technique, and the foot-in-the-door technique. In the end of the chapter, you will get to learn about the principal of consistency.

• The fourth chapter of the book focuses on the importance of social validation in our lives. It explains the importance of social validation, social proof and the principal of liking. Then it goes on to explain the importance of the influence of authority. How authority can be obtained and how it can be exercised to fulfill our obligations and achieve our goals. At the end of the chapter you will find a detailed debate on the topic of scarcity. You will learn how you can be able to play the technique of scarcity and shape people's minds and opinion. Some common techniques include the Limited Number technique, the Deadline technique and the high demand technique.

• The fifth chapter, which also is the last chapter of the book, explains in-depth the methods for how to talk to people to leave a considerable influence over them. You will be able to know what words you should use in order to make an impact. You will also get to know what words you will need to avoid so that the listener may not get annoyed and form a bad opinion of you. Next comes the importance of probing questions and a detailed analysis of the Zeigarnik Effect. The chapter contains an in-depth analysis of the yes ladder. You will get to know how you will be able to create a ladder by which you will be able to secure yeses from the customer before getting his agreement on the thing you want them to agree. In the example, I have explained how to do that step by step. The chapter also contains certain hypnotic language patterns that people use to leave an impact on the other person. It discusses the importance of hypnotic pacing statements. Then it explains the importance of subtle hypnotic language. After that it explains how to master the art of hypnotic language. The chapter concludes with the topics of the real value and existence of reality and body language that you can use to increase the scope of your influence over people.

This book carries the right recipe to learn how to influence a large number of people. You should take inspiration from the examples in the book and use them to create your own examples. This book doesn't demand that you should have prior knowledge of the subject. You can start right from zero and then go on to learn to be the master of influencing people. Go on and explore the topics in the book. Have a happy read!

Chapter 1: Manipulation

Manipulation is a technique using which a person can indirectly control the behavior, emotions as well as relationships with other people. There are lots of people who get engaged in periodic manipulation. When we tell an acquaintance that we feel fine but in fact we are depressed, it is a form of manipulation because we are on our way to controlling the perceptions of our acquaintances and also their reactions. Manipulation has a deep connection with emotional abuse, especially in intimate relations. The word manipulation is perceived as negative when it tends to harm our emotional, physical and mental health of a person.

Manipulation in a Relationship

Manipulation tends to be highly detrimental for friendly and intimate relationships. If it continues for a while, it leads to poor mental health and in some cases, to the death of a relationship. As far as marriage is concerned, manipulation may lead one partner to feel bullied and worthless. It is a fact that bad relationships have the problem of manipulation, but healthy relationships also give room to manipulation, especially when one partner intentionally manipulate the other to ease out a tense situation, kill the chances of confrontation, and attempt to lift undue burden from the shoulders of the other partner. In many cases, people willingly downplay the element of manipulation to save the relationship. In a relationship, manipulation takes a number of forms such as giving gifts, affection, showing a sense of guilt, exaggeration and passive aggression.

When parents try to manipulate their kids, they may make them feel guilty for one thing or another. Excessive manipulation leads kids to depression, eating disorder, and anxiety or some other mental health issues. A study shows that manipulation in a relationship begets further manipulation. If parents are manipulators, their kids are likely to nurture manipulative behavior. Some signs of manipulation in a parent-kid relationship are absence of accountability, overlooking achievements made by the kids and excessive interference in the life of kids.

In a manipulative relationship, the manipulated partner may attempt to meet up the needs of the other partner at the cost of the needs of his friends or family. Guilt as well as excessive coercion are the means by which a person attempts to secure favors such as a job, a loan or any other material benefit.

What Is Covert Emotional Manipulation?

Covert manipulation happens when a person, hungry for power, decides to have control over you by using deceptive methods to make you change your mind, amend your behavior as well as perceptions. Emotional manipulation takes place under the cover of your conscious awareness and has the power to make you mentally captive. Victims of emotional manipulation cannot sort out what is happening with them because it is just so covert.

A person who is skillful in emotional manipulation, makes you hand over your emotional well-being into his hands. Once you do that, he will feed on your self-esteem until you are devastated.

In-Depth Different Manipulation Techniques

If you say that you are clean of manipulating others, you are telling a white lie. We have to use manipulation at one or the other point in our lives. It can be a lie to ease out a certain situation or just a few sentences of flattery to get a job done. Let's take a look at some common techniques that are used by manipulators.

Lying

Manipulators have one habit in common and that is to lie to other people. They use this weapon to wrong-foot people and to confuse them. Lying is mostly used by psychopaths. Sometimes they opt to keep a certain part of the story hidden in order to put the victim at a disadvantage.

Devaluation

Manipulators deploy the technique of love bombing. They will make you realize that this is going to be the best relationship ever. When you are fully convinced that they truly love you, they will suddenly leave you without any explanation.

Playing the Victim Card

Manipulators often take up the role of a victim for gaining sympathy and compassion from the people who are around them. That's how they can attract you because human beings, by nature, try to get close to the people who are suffering.

They Will Target the Victim

When a manipulator stands exposed in front of people, he tries to accuse the victim to cover up his own wrongdoings. By targeting the victim, he will be able to hide his manipulation.

Gaslighting

Gaslighting is a common technique for manipulating other people. Manipulators ask a variety of questions such as 'You are crazy to say so,' and 'It is in your imagination.' It is perhaps the most insidious technique that sucks at your confidence and the power to feel justified. There are some ways to avoid it and defeat it by grounding yourself in reality and by jotting down things as they had happened. Also, you can open up and discuss it with a close friend. One of the top choices is to contact a support group who can help you recover from this disastrous situation.

Projections

Sometimes manipulators want to blame you for all the bad things that are happening to them. Everyone does that once in a while but psychopaths make it a routine business. Psychologists say that this is a kind of mechanism on the part of psychopaths who want to extricate themselves from the guilt of possessing negative behavior by linking them to someone else's behavior. If you detect anything similar in the behavior of someone close to you, don't shower any compassion on that person. Instead keep a strategic distance from them. (Stillman, n.d)

How Do You Deal With Emotional Manipulation?

There are lots of people around us who are always fabricating a plot to manipulate others by making them feel ashamed of themselves or by snatching their happiness from them if they don't follow their injunctions. Emotional manipulation is quite hurtful for people. Let's see some of the brilliant ways to deal with this problem.

Don't Open up Your Heart in Front of an Emotional Manipulation

People sometimes say, 'I am quite sad to hear that you would think that I forgot your wedding anniversary.' These words make us feel guilty even when we have done nothing to hurt others. There is nothing left to say or apologize to them. You don't have to feel guilty and you should not say anything to those people. The key is not to take care of what they are saying or doing. When you are dealing with an emotional manipulator, you should trust your gut and senses. Manipulators are always looking for a hint and once they find that weak spot, they keep hitting that.

In the above example, you asked the manipulator if he had forgotten your wedding anniversary or remember it? In response to that, they made quite a dramatic scene by putting the guilt on your shoulders for just asking this question.

Emotional Manipulator Is a Always Willing to Help

Some emotional manipulators are always looking for something they can agree to. When you ask them for help, they will take deep sighs to show as if what you are asking them to do doesn't suit them. When you ask them that it doesn't seem like they want to do what you are asking them to, they will turn the tables on you, saying how unreasonable you are for thinking so. If he agrees to do that, hold them accountable for what they do and how they do that. Don't further delve into the details. If you feel that they don't like to do that, ask them to stop. If this is not possible, go take a hot shower or a stroll on a lonely pavement, covered in autumn leaves. Enjoy what nature has to offer. (Harmer, n.d)

Emotional Manipulators Tend to Fight in a Nasty Way

Emotional manipulators like to keep things really nasty. They won't hesitate to backbite you, and also coerce and manipulate others to tell you what they wouldn't have said otherwise. One of the easiest things to note about them is that they won't show active aggression. Instead, they will be highly passive in demonstration of anger. Also, they will create pathways to let you know how unhappy they are with you. For example, they will convince you that they will support for your new job yet when you join and have to consume lots of time on office work such as creating power point presentations and charts or graphs, and get busy as a beaver in the work, they will play loud music in the home or watch TV late at night. If you dare ask them about the reason for this behavior, they will go on with their excuses and say you just cannot expect life to stop. They can be so much annoying to say the least that at times, you will want to strangle them that will land you in jail.

How to Spot a Manipulator

It feels like hell to be emotionally manipulated. Emotional manipulation is considered as highly destructive, which is why it is vital that you know how to recognize a manipulator in your life. The feat is not as easy as you might think because manipulators are skilful in what they doing. Gradually, as they see positive results, they will keep raising the stakes over time. They will be doing their job and you won't even realize what is happening. If you know the signs of an emotional manipulator, you can easily detect them around you.

They Will Play With Your Grasp of Reality

Emotional manipulators are skilled individuals when it comes to crafting lies. They will make you realize that something didn't happen when in reality it had happened. They attempt to influence our sense of reality. They are so good at doing that they we end up questioning our own selves whether what they are saying is right. In fact, we start doubting our own sense of reality that ultimately causes confusion. If you spot someone attempting to change your perception of reality, you should insist that it all sits in their imagination, and that it has nothing to do with reality. Don't let it overcome your senses.

They Will Play the Victim Card

Emotional manipulators can be easily detected because of the fact that they attempt to play the victim card more often. Whatever is becoming wrong in their life, they try to blame it on someone else. One or the other person finds himself in hot water when manipulators get caught up in an incident, because they start complaining that they have been wronged. They think that if they are unable to do a job, it is someone else's fault for setting high expectations.

They Will Not Hesitate to Hit at Your Weak Spots

Emotional manipulators always know about your weak spots and they won't stay back to push them when they get an opportunity to do that. For example, if you are worried about losing your hair, they will pass a comment on it in front of strangers or the girl you want to marry. If you are insecure about your color, they will not hold back on discussing the same in front of everyone. If you have to prepare a project to present at the office, they will try to discourage you and intimidate you by pointing out how the participants will judge you and question you. That's how they can shake your confidence and make you feel bad about the other day.

Early Warning Signs of Psychological and Emotional Manipulation

Psychological manipulation is done through mental distortion as well as emotional manipulation in order to seize power and gain privileges at the expense of the mental peace of the victim. Here are some tricks that manipulative people keep up their sleeves for coercing others and push them into a disadvantageous position. There is a difference between habits and manipulation, but it is you who must be able to recognize it.

When someone is trying to manipulate you, he will try to make you speak first. He will try to ask you inquisitive questions that would establish a baseline about how you think or behave. This helps them evaluate your strengths as well as weaknesses. If someone is asking too much questions that you find properly crafted and planned first, you are being targeted as the speaker might have a hidden agenda for doing that. This kind of psychological manipulation can happen in an intimate relationship or at the workplace with a colleague. The best course to take is to listen to them, check their behavior, and answer well-thought replies until you are able to tell if the person is doing that intentionally or by habit.

People also try to manipulate you by intellectual bullying as well. Some people consume considerable time on collecting facts and figures about a number of things in order to be an expert. Also, they want to be more knowledgeable in different areas. In fact, they want to show everyone that they are the experts in a certain field or more than one field. Not bad if they have studied hard and authentic facts, but the problem is that they advocate alleged statistics and facts, and also incorporate other data in their speech that is alien to you. They attempt to download from their brain such information that you don't have access to. If they are doing that for educating you, you will know from gestures and expressions. Manipulators hope that they are able to impose their agendas on you. By exhibiting themselves as experts, they will use this technique for no other reason than to make you feel inferior, unsettle you, and then use you for their personal benefits.

People at the helm of affairs in the government sector and the corporate sector love to entangle people into a web of paperwork and red tape. They use their position to manipulate others into submitting to something they dislike. Bureaucrats also use their influence to delay any kind of fact finding into their wrongdoings in the office.

How to Handle Manipulation

Manipulators can be your parents, intimate partners or even kids. There is no solid definition of a manipulator which makes it hard to handle. You can tell that you are being manipulated if you are losing power in a relationship, and also when conflicts are replete with emotional factors.

The first principle to deal with a manipulative person is to feel safe in a relationship. If you are not feeling safe anymore, you ought to develop a plan for maintenance of your health. You need to find a person whom you can trust and who is there to listen to your explanations. If an intimate relationship is failing in making you safe, you should remove yourself from that environment temporarily or even permanently if things don't appear to be coming back on track. Tell your intimate partner or a family member that you will not tolerate their screams and that you will not come back to their home until they stop shouting at you. Try out the following things:

1. Lock your door to cut off communication.

2. Get yourself out of the apartment.

3. Stop the car if you are driving and he is shouting at you unendingly.

4.   Refuse to accompany that person in the car.

5.   Pack up and leave the apartment to live in a hotel or with a friend.

You should wait for the right time to talk if you must initiate a conversation with the person who is manipulating you. When you think that the boundaries have been crossed, you should freeze for a moment to decide on the limits once again. You may choose not to escalate a tiny argument into a big one.

When your partner feels rejected, it is not the right time to initiate a conversation. If you are ready to confront the manipulator but you also know that the person is vulnerable to your threats such as leaving the apartment, you should wait for the right time to initiate the discussion. Confront them when they are in the state of listening. Then expose them. If the manipulator happens to be one of your parent, you should walk cautiously. Don't do anything in haste. Usually parents are not expecting this kind of behavior from their kids that's why you have to keep the tone of voice moderate. Especially if they aged, they won't be able to sustain any aggression. Speak with reasoning.

Another top tactic to handle manipulators is to take a non-combative approach for fighting back whenever you get attacked. You cannot take out anything productive by arguing so give your partner time to speak. Listen to them in a calm state and try to absorb what they are saying, and then react to it in a sensible and calculated manner. It is not easy to state your point of view when the other person is making exaggerations or exhibiting emotional intensity. Amidst all this remember one thing that you can always say a big 'No' to something you don't approve of.

Chapter 2: Dark NLP – Persuasion

The basic idea behind the development and study of Dark NLP is that people don't have any concrete identity and they have a lot of characters to take up. Dark NLP means that the fluidity of identity of a person offers a gateway for manipulators. This fluidity pushes them to adopt a personality that manipulators are looking for. They start behaving as per the will of others. This pushes them into a circle of malicious influence by manipulators who use their dark spells on them.

Seeking Truth

Stoicism has a few central teachings such as it reminds us about how unpredictable our world can be and how short time span our life has. How we can be strong and how we can take control of ourselves are the questions that everyone needs answers to. It deals with perhaps the greatest problem of our life that is the absence of logic. We usually get carried away with the flow of our impulsive behavior that entertains our senses rather than logical reasoning.

Stoicism is different from the other schools of thought in that it is practical and is not concerned with just our intellectual faculties. To succeed in the world, we must be able to do things that we would not have done in normal situations. Most of us don't try to do things that they should be doing in order to succeed in life perhaps due to the fear of unknown.

Most people trust things as they are appearing to their eyes without realizing the fact that the reality can be way more different. We should be seeing things in our surrounding as they would be, had we not been there. Our surroundings demand that we focus on what feel they are giving off such as how they are looking. The effect the sun light or the artificial light has on those surroundings can be a subject to study. You should closely observe the movement, the animals and the landscape of the place you are in. Notice the soundscape of the area.

When you are able to keep your focus on this, you will observe that a unique sense of simplicity will arise out of it. Things will appear to be more poignant. Try to disconnect from your surroundings to see the real form of things. Most people have formed a habit of looking at their surroundings through the lens of how it is going to affect them. This affects our judgment of things. We try to form a connection of things to our lives to assess whether they will fit in or not in our lives. For example, a luxury car belonging to a person will make you realize that you don't own one. When a person is taking off a holiday, it will make you realize that you don't have a holiday. That's a self-centered and self-referential lens. You should better avoid that to see the truth behind things.

The problem behind why we don't see the truth is that we don't want to see things as they are. Short glimpses of things as they are, are always there for you. All you need is to disentangle yourself from your own self and then see things as they ought to be. In simple words, we should be objective when observing our surroundings. Subjectivity colors our judgment and we can only see things in relation to how they are affecting us and not how they, in reality, are.

When we adopt this attitude, we are able to see things in a broader perspective. Every scene we will see will carry a unique signature and a unique identity to express. Even a parking lot has a unique identity to offer if you don't see it as a space for your car to stay for a while. This practice can be applied to the people around you. Notice them as if they don't have any connection with you and you will see their true self.

Making a Good First Impression

When we meet someone, it takes a few seconds to judge his personality and evaluate him. You will form an opinion of him and the other person is also doing the same during the time of your meeting. We forget the latter part most of the time. He will take notice of the dress that you are wearing, your gestures, your mannerisms, and also the way you have done your hair. Each day we meet new people who try to evaluate us and form impressions of our personalities. There is a common saying that the first impression is the last impression. It is a truth because once a person has concluded the process of calculating the first impression of your personality, he is unlikely to alter it or reverse it. Without a doubt the first impression sets the tone for the relationship. Thankfully, we can learn some smart techniques to create a brilliant first impression.

Be Punctual

You are on your way to inking a business deal and you have to meet your business partner for the first time in a hotel. If you make an excuse that you are going to be half an hour late, the other person is not going to be interested in your excuse for getting late. Even if he waits for you and finally signs a deal, he will have it in his heart that you are not a reliable person. Schedule your time as such to reach a few minutes earlier than expected. You should keep in mind the possible delays such as a traffic jam, and work on it to cut down on delays and be on time for the meeting. (Making a Great First Impression, n.d)

Be Original

Making a good first impression means that you ought to blend in with the other person for a while. It doesn't mean to lose yourself or pretend to adopt a fake personality. The best possible way to make a lasting impression is to be yourself in front of the person you are meeting for the first time. In this way you will not have to wear a fake persona each time you meet him. You will feel more confident, build solid trust and also earn respect as well as integrity from your partners.

Small Talk

If you don't open communication with the other person, it is impossible to create an impression. What topic you choose for small talk, what tone you are using, what words you select to express your thoughts matter a lot when it comes to starting a conversation. Take a couple of minutes to learn about the person. Talk more about his interests and likings. Try to know him. (Making a Great First Impression, n.d)

Building Rapport

Rapport is generally a two-way connection between different people and it must stay so. It is not something you can create yourself. In fact, you can learn how to stimulate it by following some simple steps. The very first thing to look after when you are trying to build a rapport is to give a check to your own appearance. It will help you form a connection with people. It must create a barrier. You can choose a dress that is slightly better than the dress that the other people are wearing. You should go for a modern dressing arrangement. If you think that you have excessive dress layers, remove some clothes to suit the situation. You won't want to be the butt of all the jokes cracked in a party.

Some Basics to Take Into Consideration

When you are communicating with someone, you should keep in mind the following basic elements.

- You need to express yourself as culturally appropriate. Criticizing a particular culture or talking too much about cultural taboos will present your persona as a culturally inappropriate person that is not good for business and other social matters as well.

- You should wear a smile on your face when you are communicating with the other person.

- One important thing to keep in mind is to remember the other person's name when you are communicating with him. It helps you build up a more personalized approach toward them. This brings us to Dale Carnegie's best seller book 'How to win friends and influence people.' Carbine argues that the key to win the hearts of the other people is to remember their names and then addressing them by the name when you meet them in future.

- When you are talking to someone, you should hold your head in an upright position and also maintain a good and confident posture.

- The key to building a good rapport is listening carefully to what others are saying to you. You should be attentive to the minutest of the details they are trying to discuss with you.

- The most amazing thing is not to overstay your welcome at any place you go. Don't let others get fed up with your presence.

Elements of Communication

There are three different elements of communication to make a killer first impression. Let's analyze them.

Mirroring: The first of all in Natural Language Processing technique is mirroring. This suggests that a person's behavior should match that of the others so that there should be no barrier in the communication. When the other person doesn't remain comfortable in talking to us because our behavior is making him reluctant, a communication gap is a must to build up. Mirroring helps us overcome such barriers.

Controlling the flow of conversation: This is yet another important element in conversation. We have to learn to control the flow of our conversation. It is not anything such as dictating other people or simply overpowering them in the conversation. The main objective is to fully engage the listener into what you are talking about. It doesn't mean that you start being coercive in the communication, but instead you should be able to engage the other person into the idea that you are trying to download from your brain.

Setting expectations: Once I met a client to ink a business deal. We had a good chat in the half-an-hour meeting that we had. The next day I texted her to inquire about a missing point in the proposal and to know whether she wanted me to include it and email her the updated proposal. I expected her to respond in ten minutes but she didn't reply until I sent a second text around eight hours later. During those eight hours I kept thinking if that person liked me or not or if she was considering my proposal or not. I had set wrong expectations and this kept me on the edge. We should set expectations to the minimum and as natural and logical as we can whenever we see a new person. This is minimize undue pressure on our nerves.

How to Set Expectations

This section contains a short step by step guide on exactly how you can set expectations in any conversation. The very first step is to understand that it is very hard to set and then fulfill expectations. You should be able to verbally articulate or write on a piece of paper about the expectations you have for the other person. The next step is to know when you should set expectations such as the time during the conversation when you need that. How to communicate or when to communicate them?

You need to help people see the bigger picture. They should know the 'why' factor behind the expectations that you are trying to set. When they understand the reason behind setting expectations, they are likely to fulfill them. For example, you are expecting them to finish a job in a thirty minutes timespan. You should tell them why it is important to finish the job in a short window of time. Once they know the 'why' factor, you have successfully set the right expectations.

When you are done with the initial steps of setting expectations, you should move on to have a couple of meetings with the other person to discuss about the expectations that you have set to know whether they are on schedule or not and also how they are approaching the said project.

You should be regularly conversing with whom you have set your expectations. They may have expectations from you. The ideal scenario is that both of you get your expectations fulfilled. Better for business and long-term commitment.

It is always a good idea to bring your expectations into written form as written things offer us greater clarity. Unwritten things are dependent on our memory that's why chances are high that we may forget them.

The last step is to get agreement from the other person that he will fulfill his expectations. Also, give your agreement to the other person that you will fulfill all the expectations that the other person has set for you. This kind of mutual understanding will boost up confidence in your relationship.

Expectations can be set and fulfilled by mutual agreement. Usually, we fail in communicating what we expect from others in a lucid way. This ambiguity takes its toll on our relationship. When the ambiguity is completely removed, the next step is to stay committed to what you have agreed upon. This builds up the base for a long-term relationship. Good for business!

Persuading With Emotion and Pain

The most prevalent behavior among people is that decisions should be based on logic. We love to be rational because we think this kind of behavior will help us succeed in life, but we forget along the way how much power emotional persuasion has. There are particular emotions that help in persuasion. On top of all of them is sadness. It is a kind of emotional pain that is characterized by the feelings of loss, helplessness, sorrow and disadvantage. Sadness slows down the pace of decision-making. It creates a fog in your brain and compels you to make decisions that are viable only for a short-term. In addition, sad people are spontaneously drawn toward happiness. If you have the ability to appeal to their sadness, you can persuade them and influence their decisions.

Anger is another emotion that you can use to persuade people. It can be defined as an intense emotional response. It suggests that the basic boundaries of a person have been violated. Latest studies suggest that angry people are more capable of analyzing things and also distinguish between weak and powerful arguments. In the moment of anger, you are more in control of things, experts believe. If the amount of stress is reasonable, it will give a major boost to your optimism.

If you take a look at different marketing campaigns, you will know how business strategists are using these emotions to persuade people into buying their products. When you appeal to a person's emotions, you are on your way to creating a lasting connection with them that brings them in the perfect state to respond to your calls to action. When the connection has been established, they can understand what you are trying to convey to them, and they will accept it as well.

You should understand how it is working on you. Analyze a couple of businesses and charities and see what emotions they stir up inside you. Think of the ad of a company that provides controlling services for roach infestation in houses. Think about the picture of a roach getting killed by an employee from the pest control company. What emotions does this billboard stir up in you? It should be a combination of anger, anxiety and happiness. You get angry and anxious because you recall how much destruction these roaches have brought to your home, but finally you become happy that the pest control company is going to get rid of it. This will compel you to follow their call to action. You are easily persuaded when the marketing campaign played with your emotions.

What Motivates People?

Active listening is a skill that you can acquire and also develop with untiring practice, but most of the time it is a difficult skill to master as it takes considerable patience and time. Active listening means that you should fully concentrate on what is being said to you instead of just hearing what the speaker is saying. It involves use of all your senses. You can show the speaker that you are an active listener with the help of verbal as well as non-verbal messages. The most common gestures are eye contact, smiling, nodding and saying yes or no in order to encourage them to continue. There are different gestures and signs that show that a person is actively listening to what is being said.

Smile: some people express their tendency to actively listen to the speaker by passing slight smiles off and on. You can pair up your smile with the nod of your head to make them more meaningful.

Eye contact: if you are looking to the sides, the speaker will take it as a non-attentive gesture. Eye contact is a must to show the speaker that you are actively listening to him. However, in some cases, eye contact can be intimidating for a shy speaker. You have to determine how much eye contact you need to make an impact. For leaving a healthy influence, you should add a couple of smiles to the eye contact.

Posture: your posture tells a great deal of details about your personality and habits. Attentive listeners develop the habit of leaning forward while they are listening. Active listeners also tend to give a slant to their heads.

Earning the Right to Ask a Question

Have you ever wondered how a salesman sell products to a big number of people? He carries solutions to the problems of people. Selling is not about convincing people into purchasing a product. Instead, it is about tracking down what people want and then providing them with the same. It is about helping people manage their lives in a better way. When an entrepreneur is producing a product, he has to keep certain questions in his brain. He has to ask the right questions from himself. If you don't ask the right questions, you don't know what the needs of the buyers are and how you can fulfill them.

Answering Questions With Questions

If we talk in general, people don't like a question in response to a question as an answer. But doing that has significant advantages. Perhaps one of the best feelings is that it relieves the pressure off your back and diverts it to the one who is asking the question in the first place. It helps because as long as you have to answer questions, you will be on the defensive side and you will have to feel the discomfort attached to answering questions. By throwing a question in response of a question, you will push others into the same situation in which they gave pushed you earlier on. Some questions are less a question and more an attack on the listener to unsettle him. This method is the best to take the heat off of you and channelized to the speaker. This method will also help you set the tone and the temperature of the conversation you are having with the other person. If you are answering a question with a question in response, you are on your way to get an answer that you would otherwise not have achieved. This is how you can get yourself out of stick situations by answer tough questions with questions.

Softening Statements

This section highlights how to soften your harsh statements or questions using a simple technique. One day I rushed to a bank to pay my bills as I had to take a flight to Los Angeles where my daughter and wife waited for my arrival. We had planned a vacation together. The line at the billing counter was a pretty long one. I broke the line and approach the cashier while a woman, who had been there for quite some time, stood there and saw what I was doing to her. She waited for a full minute before shouting at me and asking me what I was doing. "What do you think you are doing young man?" she almost shrieked into my ears. I took a glance around me to see who she was and why she was shouting at me. It was then that I realize that I had broken the line. When I heard the shout, I got mad and I really wanted to do the same to her, but I held back and asked the cashier to help her first. This really calmed her down and her anger vanished into thin air in a matter of seconds. She was an old woman. I realized that I would be in her place someday. Yelling is normal to many households. I grew up in the house of yellers. My parents and siblings loved to do that and it was not always done in anger. Yelling refers to the tone of our voice, but a sharp sound appears to be really harsh and brash. I got used to it as I spent around twenty years listening to this.

I had married to a calm and peaceful girl who would loved to convey her messages in a polite tone. Kirstin was a beautiful lady who would calm me down whenever I happened to burst out in anger. She advised me to lower down my voice tone whenever I was in anger. She believed that a calmer tone really helps in settling down a hyper situation. That day in the bank I remembered her instructions. I handled the situation by responding in a polite manner to yelling and anger, and consequently it helped me defuse a charged situation, saving me from unwanted embarrassment. I was happy for myself because I was able to deal with situations in a calm manner.

All this happened because I transformed harsh statements into soft statements and it worked pretty well. If you want to skilfully handle charged situations, you should be able to soften somewhat harsh words and tune them to normal. For this purpose, you will have to bring some changes to your personality. The first is to admit that your approach was wrong. I admitted to the lady that I had done wrong by breaking the line, and I should not have done that. The admission of doing wrong melts the hearts of people who even have a heart like a rock. The second and the final change is to submit to accountability. In my case, I was accountable to my wife whom I had empowered to snub me and chastise me whenever I got off the right track. (Mobley, 2014)

Let's take a look at some common examples of softening harsh statements into soft ones. Often, companies use the word downsizing instead of laying off when they are wrapping up their man power. In this way loss of jobs doesn't sound negative. This technique is known as euphemism in English literature. English novelists were fond of using this technique.

Finance companies nowadays use the following words when they are revealing their forecast for the next few months. Their director may say that they had reduced the forecast for the second quarter, but the word 'reduce' sounds negative and it will leave a negative effect on the stock market. Instead, they say that they had adjusted the forecast for the second quarter.

Instead of saying that the company has decided to cut salaries by 2%, they would say that the company has decided to cut down costs or control expenditures. These kinds of softening statements help business improve their image. Better for their business! Softening statements are like a magic spell as they calm down hyper sentiments and anger and project a positive image of an individual and a company.

They are often used in the stock market business. Investors and traders use the word 'negative sentiments' when the stock market nosedives. Apart from that when a particular stock is lagging behind the others, they say that the stock is going through corrections after a rally instead of saying that the stocking is shedding value or is coming down the hill. If you take a look around certain business campaigns and news, you will get to know that business across the word vigorously follow this technique.

Chapter 3: How to Influence People

The world is a complex place to live in and survive. Only the fittest can survive and nowadays being fit means being able to wield a massive influence over people so that people are ready to listen to you and forgive your wrongdoings. If you are a manufacturer, you cannot sell a product unless you learn the trick to influence people and change their minds.

In this chapter I will explain how you can be able to influence people and what its benefits are. You will learn about a number of methods that can be used to shape the opinion of others in your favor.

Brainwashing

Brainwashing is often referred to as a thought reforming and a well-planned technique to influence a person's behavior, beliefs and political opinion. The term has its origin in the United States, surfacing in the military circles when a big number of American military prisoners defected to the communists after getting captured by the Korean military. The soldiers were returned to the United States but the military high-ups were alarmed to learn that the American soldiers were not thinking and acting the same way as they had been trained. A few of them had been harboring anti-America doctrines and had been appreciating the Marx methods to rule over a nation. It all happened during their incarceration period. Experts found out later on that the soldiers were subjected to sleep deprivation and psychological manipulation that are broke down their personality and autonomy.

Nowadays, the United States and other countries who are at war against terrorism believe that the same tactics are applied on the people that are used by religious organizations. We call these people extremists and terrorists. This helps us understand why a sixteen years old teenage girl, who has so much to see and do in life, jumps into a crowd of people and blows herself to pieces in a terrorist attack.

Brainwashing is considered as an invasive form of influence and it demands full isolation which is why it is possible in prisons and in terrorist camps that are mostly isolated from civilized society. It is crucial for the agent to exercise complete control over the target in order to conclude the brainwashing session in a conclusive manner. By complete control, I mean the control over his sleeping patterns, eating schedule, washroom and bathroom needs and any other basic human need such as the need for some fresh air. Once the agent successfully wipes out the data on the brain of the target, he replaces it with a set of beliefs, behaviors of which the target had previously no knowledge.

Some psychologists say that brainwashing is possible under the right conditions while others consider it as a milder form of influence than the media considers it to be. Some definitions of brainwashing demand that the presence of a threat of physical harm is imminent in the brainwashing session while others say that there is a type of brainwashing that don't rely on nonphysical coercion as a means of influence. Experts do believe that the effects of brainwashing to influence others stay for a short span of time. They believe that the popular belief that the target loses his unique identity when he embraces the new planted identity is not right as his true identity is not completely lost but is pushed down into hiding inside the brain. Once the agent stops reinforcing the new identity, the target will recover his old behavior and beliefs. So the verdict is that the agent must reinforce the new identity of the target in a regular manner. (Layton, n.d)

Influence People

You have influence power so do everybody else has. It is the ability to motivate as well as inspire the masses to take action. The power of influence is what makes you stand out among the rest of the lot. This is the major difference between a leader and a manager. Influence, in general, refers to one's ability to exert a positive effect on others in order to convince others to gain support. When you are able to exert influence on other people, you get the power to persuade them and engage them toward an idea.

It is the application of power for gaining the results that you want or to achieve certain objectives for yourself or for an organization. Experts believe that people try to use some key techniques such as logical reasoning, socializing, exchanging, consulting, building alliances and modeling. At the same time there are some dark sides of influencing others such as intimidating, avoiding, manipulating and threatening.

Experts also believe that influence is not an easy feat to pull off. We exercise influence over our kids, partners, and friends and at a bigger level, countries exercise influence power over other nations. The power to influence others is always inside us. All we need is to unleash its potential and reap its benefits. It is a fact that we need a little bit of polishing. Whenever we attempt to affect how most people think and behave or make a decision, we are exercising our power to influence them. Similarly, a smile and even a simple handshake help us socialize with people and influence their opinion. Whenever we break down barriers with strangers, we get into a position to influence them. If you want to know whether people are getting influenced by you or not, you should see if they like you and your thoughts. If they do, they have already been influenced by you. All you need is to kick off the process and get it going. Gradually, you will realize that they wouldn't be able to say 'no' to your requests.

The top rational approach to influencing people is logical persuasion of other people. You should use logic to explain what you need to believe and what you want others to believe. People sometimes are greatly attracted toward logical persuasion. You should tell them what you think about a particular business or an idea. When you communicate with them, they get a chance to your opinion and your thought process. That's how they are likely to appreciate your thoughts, and when they do that, you have got the power to influence them. They will listen to what you say and very possibly do what you want them to do.

Socialization is another tool that is brilliant when it comes to influencing others. By socializing with different people, we get a chance to be open as well as friendly with them. We can talk about their achievements and appreciate them. We can also appreciate their thoughts and opinions that allows us to bring them into our friend circle. The trick is a simple one. We should keep in mind that every person on the planet loves to hear his reasonable praise that's why when we are appreciating someone for a reason, we get great influence over them, which we can use later on.

Another popular technique that we normally use is asking questions from people when we are trying to initiate a project or launching a scheme for our business. Engaging others into giving their input is a brilliant way to bring them into your magical circle of influence. People love when you give them importance and request them to leave their input for your projects. They like to express their opinion on the pros and cons of a particular scheme and how it will affect your business. If you ask them to pass a review on your business project, they will appreciate you and form a positive image of you in their brains. That's where your power to influence them starts. They will listen to whatever you say.

The power to influence can be lethal in the hands of manipulators. Manipulators also use some common but dark techniques to negatively influence others. They will force others to act against their best interests. To accomplish this objective, they will avoid their responsibility and put it on the shoulders of other people. They can use deceit and lies to attain their objective. Also, they will be seen disguising their intentions and withholding certain information.

Manipulators also try to impose themselves on other people by forcing them to comply by using loud voice, arrogance, abrasion and insensitivity that is a preferred technique for bullies. The most heinous technique they can use is to threaten other people to harm them in case they are unable to comply. The threats can be the show of weapons or by describing an example of someone who had been subjected to their wrath for non-compliance of their orders. This is the technique that despots and dictators have been rigorously using throughout the history of the world.

The Features That Matter in Strengthening Your Ability to Influence Others

Leaders have a unique ability to influence others. They master the skills that are needed to assume the role of a leader. These abilities include learning agility, the power of communication and self-awareness etc. If you cannot influence others, you cannot make reality what you have envisioned for the world or for those who are around you such as your family and friends. The people who want to lead don't just command over others but they also become inspiration for others. They know the art of persuading others and also encouraging others. They tend to tap the knowledge of a particular group and direct certain individuals toward some lofty goal.

Leaders should build up a politically savvy mindset. They should also build up a special skillset to view politics at a neutral level and as a crucial part of an organization. They must understand how important politics is for the health of an organization. They should do proper networking to develop their social capital that must include a special mingling strategy. Leaders should think before they respond to people, and also set goals before you decide how to express yourself. In addition, leaders should pay close attention to active listening.

Another important feature of the personality of leaders is that they maintain a robust foundation of trust among employees or followers. Leaders should learn to trust first and then demand the same from their followers or employees in an organization. That's how they are able to convince people to comply with what they say and what they demand. Trust is vital for the growth of an organization, and it helps deal with the toughest of challenges in a fruitful way.

Reciprocity

Let's start this section by understanding the principle of reciprocity. I'll go over the norms of reciprocity and how they can be utilized for powerful influence. I'll show you how to think about applying reciprocity to your own attempts to influence people.

The principle of reciprocity is the basic of foundation of a relationship. It can be defined as one of the most crucial human needs to give back something they have received from the other end of the relationship. When I was a kid, my friend gifted me an expensive fountain pen on my fifteenth birthday, a couple of days before the party. I wasn't used to receiving expensive gifts from friends in that way, but I was really happy because nothing in the list of my birthday gifts even came close to its lush and glamor. It was simply brilliant. The friend was so selfless that he even didn't show up at the birthday party so that I might not remain under his influence because of the gift he had given to me. The birthday cake was cut and the night had gone, but I couldn't forget that pen. I had a powerful urge to return something to him before I started using the pen, and I did exactly that. I didn't use that pen until I gifted him an equally expensive wrist watch. It is human nature that whenever we receive something from person who doesn't had given it without expecting anything in return, the urge in us to return the favor gets the strongest.

If you take a closer look at the world around you, the world is full of reciprocities. When someone takes a favor from his colleague, he returns it with a thank you. The communication doesn't stop there. The person who receives it, returns the favor with a welcome, and it happens on a daily basis. Our brain is naturally wired to return something in exchange for what we receive. Just imagine a girl who has been receiving gifts from her girlfriend for one year but has not reciprocated the favors. Will they friendship last till the end of the world? It is hardly likely that it will. Only the relationships that are built on the principles of reciprocity tend to last for a while. Also, they last until the principle of reciprocity is violated. The same principle works between a buyer and a seller.

You can integrate the principle of reciprocity into your personality and it will help you maintain a healthy and powerful influence over other people. The best strategy is to give something to others without expecting anything in return from them such as a discount and a bonus. If you are businessman and sell a product, you will be able to double up your customer base by using this method. You can offer some gift or some other incentive such as a 'buy one get one free' thing on your product. Also, in return of the package or the favor, ask the customers to leave an email or a message on social media in praise of the products or services of your company. You can offer them access to emails, social media groups or any other forum where they can easily leave their feedback.

You can also thank your customer in reciprocity when you have sent the order. You should take up a personalized approach for thanking your customers. Address them by their name and be specific about the product or service they have requested. Then go on to thanking them from the core of your hearts. That's how you can build a positive image of your brand and also make yourself highly influential.

The Pre-Giving Technique

Pre-giving is the most basic reciprocity technique, and it involves a very simple way of gaining influence. The basic idea at work behind this technique is that when you give someone a physical gift, you will be able to secure favors from them in return. Your likelihood of exercising healthy influence on them increases. Even if the gift you are giving someone is a small one, you are basically creating an expectation that the other person will reciprocate it and that too with gratitude, just because you have made the first move. That's why pre-giving becomes highly important in terms of exercising influence over other people. It shapes up or positively contributes to our first impression on the other person.

A study was conducted to look into the technique of pre-giving and also judge how effective and beneficial it is. Participants believed that the person with whom they were interacting was just another participant while in reality he was one of the actors that researchers had hired to conduct the study. They were only pretending to be participants. In the middle of the experiment, the actors requested the other participants leave the place for a couple of minutes. When they got back, the experiment continued normally as it was getting on before. Sometimes the actor didn't return empty handed, but he had a pair of Coca Cola bottles in his hand. On entering the room, the actor told the real participant that he had brought the drink for him. So the participant received a gift from the actor just like we exchange gifts in normal days.

When the experiment ended and the two participants, one of them an actor, were packing up to leave the room, the actor told the participant that he had been selling raffle tickets and that if he sold more tickets, he would win a prize. It was like a competition so the actor asked the participant if he would buy any tickets. The researchers wanted to check the reaction of the participants.

When the results were prepared and unfolded for the public, it turned out that usually a person is willing to buy just one ticket, but the participants of the study were willing to buy two tickets on average. That was an amazing turn of events. They agreed to pay double price just because they had received a gift in the form of soda from the actor. This showed when someone gives a gift no matter how humble it is in terms of value, we are highly likely to follow his directions. This is a spontaneous reaction which sometimes we cannot explain. Reciprocity principle immediately gets into action when the person demands something from us.

There are certain elements that are crucial for the functioning of the pre-giving technique. It must be kept in mind the time span between these two things should not be extraordinary long. The shorter the time span is, the higher will the compliance level from the other person. The study showed that after the week had passed, the results were slightly different, but a month, the results had totally changed. The effect of the gift and the influence it had brought to the giver had gone into thin air. There wasn't much effect on the participant.

We can give an absolutely free gift just like the one that actors in the above mentioned experiment did. It can be a physical and a free gift. It can be in the form of free content that you offer to your customers in the form of blog posts or eBooks or email letters. When you are providing them useful information for free, you are actually making them feel indebted to you. Another method is to send wish cards to your customers to special occasions such as Christmas or New Year. All the things have the sole objective to give away something absolutely free to your customers or the people around you. The pre-giving technique turns out to be pretty much helpful in business. The key is to give away a gift then ask them for a favor in a short window of time. The favor should be a reasonable one and something that the customers can easily do. (Reciprocity technique #1: pre-giving, n.d)

An Overview of Common Persuasion Techniques

Persuasion can turn out to be a Herculean task if you don't do it right or you don't tread the right path. Convincing a single person on your viewpoint is pretty tough. Just imagine convincing a dozen or a group of fifty people. Still, there are lots of people around us who are pretty expert at convincing others, and they always leave us wondering why it happens that some people have a better ability. Have you ever met a salesman of any company? Some of them are pretty good at cracking a deal with a customer. Convincing others is their bread and butter. They have that steel confidence in their personality that they will be able to convince the people they met to sell things. Psychologists have successfully crafted certain techniques which you can use to boost up your convincing power. Let's review those techniques.

The That's Not All Technique

Although an influence tactic in the "reciprocity" family yet the That's Not All technique takes a different approach to utilizing this principle. Marketers use this technique for persuading potential customers who are still thinking about what to buy from the market. This is a special technique because of the fact that it takes into account making a request and afterwards putting great emphasis on the benefits of the product or service with the help of additional arguments before you ask the person to comply with your request. For example, your salesman is selling motorbikes at a showroom. The hall has been filled with around one hundred customers who are here to buy motorbikes. The showroom has five other companies that have put their products on display. All of them have salesperson who are actively working to sell maximum items. Your salesperson tells the customers about the benefits of buying the motorbike such as great speed, economical average with respect to consumption of oil and lots of other benefits. There is one rider who is demonstrating how the motorbike runs and how it sounds. Just before your salesman makes the call to action, he adds, "That's not all. When you buy the motorbike, you will get ten liters of gas as bonus." (Common Strategies: Common Persuasion Techniques, n.d)

Ten liters of gas is just peanuts in front of a bike that is worth several thousand dollars but the impact it makes on the minds of buyers is huge. It is a free gift from you for them. It will add great strength to your persuasive arguments.

Foot-in-the-Door Technique

The foot-in-the-door technique is a genius application of consistency norms to maximize the chances that someone will agree to do something for you. It's not as violent as it sounds--I promise! This technique involves making a little request that a person is likely to agree upon. When he agrees on the little request, you can go on to make a larger request. You can understand this by the name of the technique. When you are able to step a foot in the door, you are ready to walk through the other doors. When the buyer agrees to your first request, you can secure the right to make them agree to the second favor. Sales personnel use this technique to boost up sales. For example, the salesman for your motor bikes may ask a random customer, "Do you mind telling me which company's motorbikes you ride?" (Common Strategies: Common Persuasion Techniques, n.d)

The customer will think that he is doing a favor to the salesperson by just telling him the name of the company. He will be interested in the question thinking that the workers are doing a kind of survey to collect data about the people who are bike riders. Bike riders usually love to answer questions about their bikes. Once the first question gets an answer, the salesman can go on to ask the next question.

"Why don't you try our bikes? They are a good ride as compared to your current bike?"

Starting a conversation in this way helps you secure more clients than directly asking them to buy your product or switch to your service. A number of studies have supported this technique as the best technique for salespersons to sell different products. First make a small request and then deciding upon the response of the customer, go on to ask for a bigger favor. This strategy can be applied to any household item such as soap products, electronic devices etc.

Door-In-The-Face Technique

In one last instance of reciprocity in action, the "door-in-the-face" technique takes yet another perspective on how to take advantage of reciprocity norms. This technique is just another method to make a request that tends to operate in the back way. Using this technique, you can make an unreasonable request that the other person is going to refuse right away. This method is quite beneficial in sales negotiations. For example, a motorbike salesman, may offer a customer to trade his old bike for a new one from your company by offering the customer a tiny amount for his old bike. We know the result of this request. The customer is going to refuse it anyway as it was intended by your salesman. When he has received the refusal from the customer, he will then turn toward the customer once again and come back with another offer that is more reasonable than the last one, and that he thinks the customer will incline towards. Even if the second offer is going to be lower than what ought to be reasonable, the customer is going to accept it because he has already been subjected to a ridiculously low offer. (Common Strategies: Common Persuasion Techniques, n.d)

Experts explain that one reason behind the influence of the door-in-the-face technique is that it plays on the sense of guilt of the customer. They realize that they had already declined the initial request of the salesman that's why they should accept the second request. The sense of guilt starts getting over their nerves that they have not helped out the salesman upon the first request. When the second request is made and it also appears to be more reasonable than the first, the customer readily agrees to it. The second request offers them an opportunity to decrease the level of guilt that the customer had experienced.

There is another explanation why this technique worked, and that is the refusal of the customer to the first request gives birth to a grave concern on the part of the customer that his reputation has been torn apart. They may feel that the salesman considered them as uncharitable or somewhat rude or even uncooperative. Let me explain this in simple words. As human beings we are always looking out for a second opportunity whenever we do something wrong. The second request by the salesman turned out to be that second opportunity that the customer had been thinking about. He grabs it and satisfies himself by presenting himself as a fair person. (Common Strategies: Common Persuasion Techniques, n.d)

Low-balling

The low-ball technique is one more way of utilizing the consistency principle to maximize your influence. Using this technique involves being careful about how you present all the necessary information. The low-ball technique is about making a request to the customer and then gaining an agreement on the same from him. You have to change the terms of that deal at the nick of the time. This is an unethical method of securing agreement from the customer, but that's the way to do that.

Take the example of a motorbike salesman who may tell his customer that he is selling a bike for $15,000. The customer happily agrees to pay the price, thinking that he has received the best deal for the bike. Everything is agreed upon. The time comes to sign the agreement papers. It is then that the salesman reveals that the price he told the customer was incorrect, and now he could only sell the motorbike at $18,000. The customer had been waiting for a long time in your office, during which he has made up his mind to purchase the motorbike. That's why he agrees to buy the motorbike at a higher price. This technique also is about saving your reputation in front of the salesman and the other staff. (Common Strategies: Common Persuasion Techniques, n.d)

Consistency

The principle of consistency can be explained from the fact that people, in general, desire to be consistent in words and deeds. Can you recall an event when you had made commitment to a person but could not fulfill it? Did it make you feel good or was it a terrible experience? Most if the people consider it a bad experience. They think it is embarrassing and shameful to leave a commitment in the middle.

People, usually, are highly likely to do things in which they feel more consistent with. They adopt the attitude that they most of the time carry and feel comfortable with. Consistency is considered as an adaptive behavior that really helps when we are trying to influence others. The world is really a complex web in which only the person, who has made up habit to make decisions and do certain acts on a set pattern following a set of values, can survive.

People feel bad if they say that they will do a thing and then change their mind and say that they cannot do that. This inconsistency is also considered as an emblem of unreliability. We tend to struggle for consistency in the commitments we make. We have to keep up with our values and attitudes when we are faced with acting on some plan of action. We have to keep up with our attitudes that we have trained over the past several years.

It is human tendency to not only be consistent in reality but also be able to portray himself as a consistent person. You can do that by making public what you do. You can also talk about it in your family and friend circles. Share it with your partner and friends in addition to mentioning it in your social networks. It works two ways. When people know about our habit of being consistent, they create a sort of pressure that keeps us moving with the same level of consistency. The second benefit is that it portrays our image as a person who doesn't compromise over his principles. It will definitely add to your power to influence people. When you say something, people will be expecting that you will stand by it and that's why they will listen to you and act on what you say.

Chapter 4: Introduction to Social Validation, Liking and Scarcity

In this chapter, I'll cover the basics of social validation, including its relationship with conformity and the way psychologists have understood its effects. Social validation is the greatest way to motivate people. Let me deal with this concept by explaining what symptoms to watch for when you are seeking social validation. Each of us has to go through a certain time when we are subjected to a unique environment due to one or another reason. Sometimes it is because of our new job in a different than in which we have been living. Sometimes it is because of our studies when we have to live in a different city or country to attend a university.

If you have been subjected to a new environment, the chances are high that you might have observed what people do around you. Whenever you meet a stranger, you try to mimic their gestures and language to blend in the environment. This is our first attempt to seek social validation in a totally new place. We just don't want anyone to stare at us and call us a stranger or check our behavior.

If you look at social validation through the lens of psychology, it means that a person is conforming to a social group and also following actions of that particular group to blend in their company or simply to win their trust. Social validation is about adjusting your gestures, language and appearance in accordance with where you are going to or where you are living in. The phrase, When in Rome, do as the Romans do, can explain how social validation works.

Social validation is all about conforming to the traditions of the current environment that you are living in. Adaptation to an alien setting is a natural process and we unintentionally do it sometimes.

Social validation follows the principle of conformity. When a customer is not sure if he should go ahead and buy something, he has to rely on the reviews that other users have made on the benefits of the product. Only after that they are convinced that they reviews are great, the chances of their making the purchase considerably increase. Social validation works on the principle of liking and conformity by a great number of others customers.

Consumers are more likely to buy a product that their peers endorse to them rather than going for the product that celebrities endorse. Consumers are more likely a buy a product from Amazon if it has a good number of positive views.

The "Social Proof" Technique

This theory was first advocated by Robert Cialdini who maintains that a person who is unaware who to behave in a certain social circle, will look forward to other people. Social proof is something that help us discern what is right from the eyes of the other people. what other thinks correct becomes right in our eyes.

When we cannot judge a situation ourselves, we look out for social proof to validate our judgment. Social proof reinforces our judgment or totally reshapes it as well. Social proof works well during the time of crisis when we don't have sufficient time to think and make a decision. Social proof shapes our behavior and the theory that explores and confirms this notion is known as the Informational Social Influence Theory.

Applying social validation to the compelling influence is pretty straightforward. I'll give you some specific mechanisms of how social proof can be used and why it's so effective.

The first mechanisms is uncertainty. It is the fuel that tends to fire up and also feed the mechanisms of social proof. When we face an unfamiliar situation, we become uncertain about the result of the circumstances, that's why we feel the need to refer to our social circle for guidance on the matter. It is a kind of reassurance that we are doing the right thing.

Another mechanism is similarity that tends to motivate us and also enhance our social proof. When we identify ourselves with a group of people, we are highly likely to attend to their recommendations and suggestions. The similarity can be based on age, color, race, nationality, language, physical appearance or some job occupation. Studies suggest that we are more likely to follow the guidelines laid down by our peers with whom we share a similarity.

Social proof helps us move around our social circles without any fear of rejection or odd behavior on part of our peers. We can protect ourselves from taking actions that would make us feel alienated from the society. When a company sells a toothpaste, it includes a tagline that four out of five doctors have recommended it use. That's how they try to validate that our peers have confirmed the use of a particular toothpaste. Testimonials by someone from our social circle are more likely to click our minds than endorsement by celebrities.

There are some dangers of social proof as well, and they can be quite detrimental and hazardous. For example what our peers are doing is not the right thing. If we follow them blindly, we are going to land ourselves in great trouble. Social proof is considered as the most powerful weapon to persuade and influence people. If we use it in the right way, we can be able to improve our personal lives and social interactions.

Liking

Why do companies hire sexy models to sell cars, energy drinks and perfumes despite the fact that it is the males who are greatly attracted toward sport cars and energy drinks? Liking is important when it comes to exercising influence over people. Customers want a website to look good to convince themselves that it is credible and likable. It should have a brilliant design and unique functions that must offer users enjoyment during the time they have to click all the buttons.

If you take a look at the website of Black Clothing, they are hardly using any high quality photos for the visitors to soothe their eyes. Instead they have uploaded a fun video at the start of the website. Users watch this video and enjoy the introduction before they enter the website and explore its pages. The video features multiple hot and beautiful models who are wearing Black Milk Clothes, and are having fun as the preparations for Christmas go on. Liking can be a powerful influence strategy. I'll further show you exactly what I mean by "liking" and why it can be such an important tool of influence. The customers who happened to like the video, are more likely to buy the products from the online store. So physical attraction does wonders when we are trying to get people to like something we want them to.

One especially useful tool for increasing your likability and aiding in your influence attempts is the similarity technique. I'll show you a few examples of this technique in action and also show you how to think about applying this strategy yourself.

This is the second principle of liking. Most of the brands that are being produced across the world fail to relate to the customers. We prefer to purchase things from a company that loves to interact with its customers and is quite empathic. When a corporation gets involved in live interaction with people, people start liking it and its products because they try to find a relationship with the company and the product. For example, Ufone, a cellular company, has created a logo Ufamily. The users of the company now boast of being a part of the Ufamily. They have found a relationship to nurture and take care of. They buy its products because the company has offered them a new identity. They like their slogan and that's why they buy their services.

Nowadays big brands are working hard to cut down on the distance that exists between the customer and the company. They have started to realize that they cannot behave like an alien or a superior being who have the responsibility to provide the customers what they cannot produce themselves. They know that they have to be a friend of you to sell their product. You have to build a kind of reliability as well as similarity. When you know that your customers can relate to you, you can better understand their problems that they face and then provide solutions in accordance with it.

Yet another tool based on liking is the familiarity tactic. You'll see a few examples of familiarity in action, and I'll also dispel some myths about what has to occur for someone to benefit from "familiarity." By using this technique, you can make a conscious effort to create familiar face prior to making a request. This strategy results in greater compliance in response to the request that you make. People are highly likely to get influenced by the ones they are more familiar with. How to create a sense of familiarity among the people is a challenge that you have to take up.

Introduction to Authority's Influence

It should come as no surprise that authority figures have huge influence. But why? And how deep does that influence run? Influence largely happens when a person or a specific group tends to affect some other person or a group. Power is the capacity of a person or a group of people to influence other people or groups. On the other hand, authority is an offshoot of power that is given in the hands of a specific individual group.

There are number of people who surround us all the time. Among them are religious leaders, doctors, teachers, police, military men and fire fighters. They are people who are in the positions of authority. They are highly revered by the masses because by nature human beings respect authority and power. When a doctor says that we should be consuming sugar, we refrain from it. When a doctor asks us to take medicine for two weeks, we abide by him because we respect what he says. Similarly, when a cop asks us to get out of the car, we respect what he says because of his authority. When a professor of a university asks us to consult a specific book, we go to the market to buy that because we respect his knowledge.

The point is that we like to rely on people whom we consider as having superior knowledge in a particular area such as a medicine, health, teaching, law or other specialized fields. People across the world get easily swayed by the influence of those who are at the helm of affairs. If you are running a business and a staff of fifty is working under your control, you are an authority figure for them. Leaders and manager must understand the principle of authority as it has turned out to be a powerful tool for exercising influences over people.

Where authority is easy to exercise, it also is easier to abuse. It is important you use it in a measured way so that you can be able to maintain your trust among employees. Once you lose the trust among the people who are under your authority, it is nearly impossible to rebuild the same. When you start exercising authority over the people, the other principles of persuasion become easier to implement. An important thing on authority is that you should not be using it for personal gain. If you do that, you will have to pay for it. You will be held accountable for that. You have to use this principle wisely and you will be happier than ever and will be able to bring about more productivity for your firm. To exercise authority over people, you have to take care of the following principles. Let's talk about them one by one.

The very first principle is of aestheticism. You have to present yourself as the one who is immensely careful of his aestheticism. How you present yourself to others is important when you are an authority figure. It has a deep impact on your staff or employees. You have to be able to look like an authority. For example, you should wear an expensive dress suit with a tie that should have a neat knot. Look like an authority figure if you want to be one.

Also, you should buy an expensive sports car that communicate to the onlookers that you possess a high status. If you cannot buy a super costly car, you should keep your old and cheap car well attended. It should be spotless and well-maintained. Always do your hair and don't forget to pay attention to self-hygiene. In short, they should be inspired by your look, and in this way they will be more ready to follow your lead. That's the way human brains are wired. Another aspect of aesthetics is that they boost up your confidence.

You have to remain engaged to exercise your authority especially on new hires in your organizations and new employees in your company. These new entrants will turn out to be a fresh start for you as a leader. You should personally help them so they can navigate through the company and absorb key information that you want them to. You should make sure that they are getting access to all the information you want them to absorb. Also, help the fresh hires to absorb themselves in the culture of your company. Also, communicate the mission, values and vision of your company to the fresh hires along with the 'why' factor behind those values and the vision. You need to welcome them in a way that shows that you are extremely excited for them to join your company.

Remember that if you want to influence people with your authority, you should walk your talk. People start getting annoyed from a person who fails to walk his talk. You need to lead by example. If you want your employees to work from 9 to 5 without a break, you should show them that it is possible by doing them yourselves. If you don't like your staff to wear jeans at the office, stop wearing them yourself.

Last but not least is that you should highlight the achievements of your employees before the other staff members. We love attention, appreciation and a round of applause. This will encourage other employees to follow in the footsteps of the high achiever. In addition, it will boost up their confidence in you as a leader. They will respect you more than ever for respecting people who work hard. It is like the reciprocity principle in terms of appreciation and respect. (Eisenhauer, n.d)

Introduction to Scarcity

Yet another influence principle is that of scarcity. I'll review the nature of this influence principle and why it does what it does. The persuasive power behind making something scarce or limited to attain is quite powerful.

The "Limited Number" Technique

One application of scarcity that you've probably seen a million times is the limited number technique. I'll review a classic study from the science of influence to discover a few refinements of the basics of limited numbers. Cialdini identified that scarcity are among the top six social influence principles that are used to elicit compliance, choice and agreement. Burger and Caldwell conducted a study to assess the impact of the principle of scarcity. They invited some participants for an experiment by making them believe that their personality test scores had been rare. They told them that they fall into the category of the top ten percent. Other participants were told that their scores were more common. The remaining participants believed that the opportunity was unique and scarce so they were more likely to show up and participate in the exercise to make it to the ten percent. In general, research alludes to creating shorting of something in terms of numbers. Just as we saw that participants came again and again in droves to be a part of a bunch of people. The scarcity of the group madly pulled them. One of the many people to make people think is that the quantity of something is reducing. When people are convinced that the number of slots or items are limited, they will be attracted toward it. (Nicholson, 2018)

High Demand

The second principle is creating a high demand. If they perceive that the demand of something is high, they move toward attaining it. In order to elicit scarcity, you need to make sure that the thing is in high demand. For example, avocado remains in high demand in the sub-continent which makes it more desirable and precious. Now apply the same principle to humans. You should develop certain habits and collect such knowledge that people are always willing to listen to you. You should also invest in yourself in terms of training so that people seek after you to gain something useful for their professional life and tips to solve their work-related issues. A person who has 100,000 followers who are ready to listen to his words is considered as highly influential. That's the reason people who have a following on Twitter, Instagram or YouTube are considered as influential. Remaining in high demand is the key to wield a powerful influence over people.

The "Deadline" Technique

Another scarcity tactic is to employ a deadline. You know this one well--or do you? It turns out that the deadline tactic isn't all it's cracked up to be, and I'll show you when this strategy can actually backfire. You can make a choice scarce by setting a time limit around it. You can put an arbitrary deadline on the option and ask people to go for it. This technique can really backfire because humans don't like restrictions. They love to be free that's why they are more comfortable in open scenarios in which they have free time to ponder over something and make a decision accordingly. If the deadline is too short, most people will fail to act thinking that they are busy and they have been subjected to injustice by being offered a short deadline. If you must set a deadline, you should create a strong call to action and keep repeating it in the ears of your customers so that they pay heed to it. One of the best call to action can be: start acting now before time runs out. (Nicholson, 2018)

Chapter 5: How to Talk

This chapter will show you how you can improve your speech that could make an impact on the masses. You will learn about certain words that you must include in your speech, words that you should do away with and techniques to use hypnotic language. You will also learn how to master hypnotic language and how you can use your body language to increase your circle of influence.

The chapter contains discussions on the Zeigarnik Effect, the Yes ladder, probing questions and pattern interrupt. You will be able to tune your speech to make it more effective and full of power.

Words to Use

Experts say that the biggest problem of the world is that we cannot persuade people to do what we want them to. We always have to confront defiance and most of the time, defiance wins. If we want to influence others and motivate them to do something, we have to convey our message in the right words. This brings us to choosing the right words to communicate our thoughts and desires. It is not just necessary for persuading people for a short while, but this ability to persuade others is also necessary for building up a good leadership quality. It demands certain stellar communication skills and also has the ability to boost up human connection. Let's go through a rundown of some magic words that can do a tremendous job while we are communicating to others.

The first word is 'Yes.' This word is a part of a lot of languages other than English. What is at the top of the fears that lots of people across the world harbor? It is the fear of facing rejection that keeps us. Our brain is wired to link the word 'no' to rejection, and that's what our brain doesn't accept. This means that the word 'yes' has a totally opposite effect on our brain. 'Yes' is perceived by our brain as a positive word and a sign of mutual understanding. If you use this word more often in your communication, you will be able to connect to the positive part of the brains of your listeners. This works perfectly well if you apply this technique on your marketing campaign. Your customer wants to be accepted by you. By hearing a streak of 'yeses,' they will be able to ease out the tension that is accumulated in their brains. Studies suggest that you should incorporate at least three yeses into your speech to make your speech effective.

The second most important word in your speech should be their name. When you call someone by their name, it means you appreciate them and value them in your life. It is the best way to win someone and bring her on your side. A person's name is the sweetest sound he can ever hear.

The most important word among all is the word thanks. Gratitude is always the most appreciated and sprightly thing that a person can ever hear. If you are running a company, you can show some gratitude to your employees by saying thanks to them for their services. It can be your first step to build a healthy relationship with your team. When the employees feel appreciated, they will be more motivated, and they are more likely to do your job in an efficient and brilliant manner. You should be ready to see considerable improvement in the time they give to your work and the level of quality they used to deliver. Similarly, you can thank your customers for buying your goods or services. The word 'thanks' will make them feel respected, productive, happy and engaged. People take enough rejections in a single day. Amidst this, a 'thanks' from you will be nothing less than a blessing for them. When you say thanks to people, they start appreciation, and the next step after appreciation is respect.

Words Not to Use

The English language contains over a million words in total. Setting aside profane words and slang, you can use all of them in your speech. Still, there are some words that you must avoid in order to successfully influence people. Let's break them down below.

The first word is 'should' which you should avoid to use in your speech. Should reveals certain weaknesses in your personality such as a weak decision making power and an absence of commitment. If you want to show the world that you are a committed person, you cannot use the word 'should.' By not using I mean you should use it where it is crucial to use, and not in any random sentence or phrase.

Another most frequent word that we speak is hope. Hope this happens. Hope that happens. Hope I become a billionaire. If we see the word in an independent position, it has a positive meaning but when we use it in different sentences, it may suggest indecisiveness, desperation and frustration. It may suggest that something is not happening despite your continuous effort. It conveys a sense of indecision. You can replace the word with desire, ambition and goal.

Probing Questions

There are lots of types of probes that you can use. They depend on what you are saying and what you want to discover. Here is a rundown different probing questions. Some probing questions are asked for a clarification. Sometimes a speaker speaks vaguely or in an extremely unclear language that needs clarification. See the following questions.

- What did you mean by that?

- What would you be doing in the coming week?

- Would you mind telling me something about this product?

Sometimes a speaker has concluded a session or is taking time to breathe for a while, and you are confused whether to walk away or to wait for them to start speaking for their second session.

- Is there anything you want to explain?

- Is that all?

- Have we reached the end of the session?

Zeigarnik Effect

If you have been a student or are a student, you can tell that your experience of revising exams might explain that concentration has the power to help you better remember certain pieces of information. Students get involved in cramming lots of knowledge and rigorous sessions of physical exercise. They will also be ready for taking a mock test before sitting in the real exam.

Up till now interruption during our work or study was considered as a bane for our work or study, but now studies have found that interruption can improve our focus and also our memory of the lesson that we were reading while we were interrupted. It was first discovered by a Lithuanian based scientist whose name was Bluma Zeigarnik. He experimented on the effect of observation and how does it get affected by certain changes and conditions of our brain. He conducted a study by which he found out that the faster a task stands completed, the least we will remember it. They linked forgetting of something to its completion in the brain. Incomplete tasks tend to stay in our brain for a longer time because our brain keeps reminding us that something is incomplete and demands our attention. For example, we remember what books we have to read and what notes we have to consult until we are done with the examination. (The Zeigarnik Effect Explained, n.d)

Zeigarnik did a number of experiment on different participants and later on found that the participants, who were interrupted during task, showed a 90% improvement in recalling things. The result suggests that when we desire a task to be finishes soon, we will remember it until we have completed it. Until we actively rehearse it, we will definitely forget it over time. (The Zeigarnik Effect Explained, n.d)

Pattern Interrupt

A pattern interrupt is used to switch the other person's strategy. All of us have patterns of behavior that have been made of the sequences of our habits. Habits affect us as an individual and also as a leader. All people have some kind of habit that they want to change. We have to do lot of things on a daily basis and these lots of jobs are done smoothly because we practice them each day. These automated habits that are an important part of our brain out of subconscious mind and the muscle memory. These habits rule over our lives. These tasks include driving a bike, drinking water, wearing clothes and combing your hair. The memory of the place where you sit to watch the television, the location of the remote control of the television. All these are automated habits. They are quite economical for us because we things start happening automatically, and they don't stress our thinking power that tends to free our mind of the burden of many things. When the brain is less engaged, it makes fast and efficient decisions.

Yes Ladder

If you take a closer look at people, you will know that each of them has created a predictable pattern to follow. If you understand them, you can use them to boost up sales revenues. This principle suggests that we have to be consistent when it comes to our attitudes and actions. The Yes ladder is considered as a top persuasion method that is aimed at getting the customer to say yes to the question that you have crafted for them. They can also say yes to a specific situation such as making a sales pitch or organizing a meeting with the customer. The process demands that you create a series of questions that would start in a trivial way but lose their triviality as you keep on asking more questions. Each of the subsequent question that they answer is likely to make them comply with the last one. That's how it goes on.

Studies say that it doesn't matter if the questions you are asking are relevant to the sales or not. Let's see how a salesman can create a Yes ladder.

Salesman: What is the name of this street?

Customer: This is Harley Street 113.

Salesman: Is it Woofer Town?

Customer: Yes, you are in Woofer Town.

Salesman: Great! Do you live in this glamorous house?

Customer: Yes, it is my house. Thanks for the compliment.

Salesman: Great! I just wanted to let you know that we are going to give away free estimates for house painting in the area. Can you find some time to come over to the Town Hall late in the afternoon or anytime tomorrow.

Customer: I'll be there tomorrow.

This is how the salesman can build the yes ladder. We have got a couple of yeses before making them agree on the real issue that is to make them willing for a free estimation of how much painting the house will cost. Let's break down the yes ladder into steps.

The first step is to identify what is going to be the big yes in your communication which in my case has been getting the agreement of the customer on a free estimate for a full house paint. It can be anything else such as sale of a car, sale of full house, sale of cleaning services or pest control services or any other thing.

The next step is building the ladder. Once you have noted down the big yes, you can then take a backward approach and initiate building the further rungs of your yes ladder. In the example, the salesman built the yes ladder by inquiring about the name of the street and the name of the town. Then he went on to get the fourth consecutive yes from the customer on getting a free estimate on how much painting his house would cost. This is a kind of building a yes compliance.

The easiest way to get the first yes to ask a random question that you already know. You have to identify something that you know the answer to. For example, our salesman asked the customer about the name of the street on which he was standing, then he inquired about the name of the town. He was sure that he would get two clear yeses by these questions. This proved to be a lubricant for the engine of our yes ladder. The important point to mention here is that you have to preplan your yes ladder, which mean that you should create questions that would get you the yeses you are looking forward to.

The last step is a bit risky as well. Each question will help you climb up the ladder and get close to your sales objective. You need to keep pushing a little more when you are climbing your way up. Before you go on to take the big risk, you need to exhaust at least three to five attempts. (Greene, 2017)

Hypnotic Language Patterns & Embedded Commands

English language is a very deep language and it has welcomed lots of revisions, grammars and words from other languages. We can structure the thoughts and put together a strong hypnotic language patterns. This may surprise many people that all of us at one time or another use hypnotic language in our day-to-day meet ups. It affects our lives and what also what we hear, see and feel, but sometimes we use it in the wrong way and bring out negative results. In this section I am going to discuss certain hypnotic language patterns you can use for fun, to boost up sales, for direct hypnosis and for seduction. Once you are on your way to understanding the structure, you can create your own pattern of hypnotic language and use it in your speech.

Hypnotic Pacing Statements

If you want to get the brains of the people feeling slippery, you should use some pacing statements. They should be true. Let's take a look at some of the statements.

And just breathe in....

As you hear what I say…

Just listen to what I am saying to you…

Get relaxed in that chair beside the stove…

If you closely observe, all these phrases and sentences have the power to touch the soul of the listener. They immediately grab the attention of the listener.

Subtle Hypnotic Language

Subtle language is considered as a powerful language. Let's see an example of a lawyer who is trying to convince the judge on the innocence of his client. Let's take a look at the following two examples and decide which one is more influential than the other.

I suggest to you that Mr. Adam is innocent.

Respected sir and the members of jury, you listened to the statement of Mr. Adam and examined the evidence. You may take the option that he is innocent in light of the evidence.

Now think which one of the above statements has greater influence than the other one? In the first sentence, the lawyer made a stubborn and lifeless assertion that Mr. Adam was innocent that fell on deaf ears. In the second example, the lawyer tried to recreate the images of Mr. Adam while he made the statement in his defense and also of the evidence that attempted to prove his innocence. The lawyer went into the details to explain his viewpoint to the jury, which helped him make an impact on the minds of the panel.

How to Master Hypnotic Language

Hypnotic language is something that is pretty difficult to master. It is nothing less than a passion to follow. People find themselves behaving as a silly person, but sounding silly is not the only hurdle in their learning process. People know the words and sentences but still they find it hard to practice in front of other people because they feel reluctant to do that. Some of them get nervous while others find it reluctant to utter the words that they are not used to speak otherwise.

The foremost technique to learning hypnotic language is to write it down and practice. Do this every other day and you will find it to be fun and a faster way to learning new skills. Like all the other things, daily practice helps polish hypnotic language. Divide your sessions in short periods with short breaks so that you may not get bored of the work. Feel no pressure and no effort at all. Instead do it in a fun way. Imagine that you are learning a new skill that is going to immensely aid you in your practical life. You need to jot down all the major hypnotic language patterns and then combine them by giving them short time to learn. See the following example.

"And the more you remember the relaxation that's within… that's right… this is just for you… now sit here… I am beginning to wonder… deep inside…from the core of the heart…… the depths of comfort… are yours to explore… so much more of the best of who you've always been… at heart…So much to say…" (Tyrrell, 2014)

Everybody Lives in a Different Reality

Quantum physics says that every one of us sees the truth in a different way, because every one of us creates what they see in their surroundings. The theory suggests that reality is not something that is carved in stone, and it is a pretty complex idea to fully grasp. Quantum physicists as well as meta-physicists have started to explore the idea more deeply than before. Everyone we meet has his own platform that gives them something to stand on. It is just like a moral standpoint that they have belief in. Their beliefs represent who they are and who they want to be as a person.

Some people believe that human race has been degenerating at a fast pace while others believe that if human race is doing pretty well. There is a massive shift in their perspectives. Some people think bumblebees might be the reason behind the food crisis that we are facing today in the world. Another person is of the belief that the problem of bumblebees takes the back seat and it is corruption that is a major issue for the world. This is proof that people are not seeing the same reality. They are living with different versions of reality.

Body Language For Influence

The way most people carry themselves can either help them in their affairs or hinder their progress. Human beings consistently give off signals from bodies all the time, which tells others how to respond to them. It also tells about their mood and character as well. The foremost of all is your smile. It is a robust to connect with the other people. Big smiles help people consider you as a confident and approachable person. People who wear a big smile are considered as warm, approachable and confident. A smile is considered as the gateway to building a strong relationship. People are always willing to help you and listen to you if they like your viewpoint. When you meet someone, it is quite important to wear a smile to look genuine. If you are not in a good mood, it is a good idea to recall a happy memory and produce a genuine smile. If a person you are talking to is not in a good mood, you can gradually develop a smile and win his heart.

When a person has a perfectly good rapport with you, it is quite easy to make them listen to your speech or your point of view. You should match your body movements with theirs. Mimic their movements and it will greatly help you feel involved. For example, when the person pick up a pen, you should pick up one too. If they put their hands on the table, you should do the same. That's how you will be able to secure a place in their hearts.

Conclusion

If I say to my girlfriend, "I like your dress" in a way that I am staring at the sky or my eyes are chasing a couple of rabbits going down the hole, she will be perturbed by the manner in which I said those words. Instead if I wear a smile on my face and make a direct eye contact, she will love it and take it as a compliment. Rolling of eyes, shaking of the head and other such gestures make us feel sarcastic and critical.

If you tend to look directly at the other person whom you are talking to, it will greatly help you communicate your sincerity and also add the flavor of directness to your communication. On the other hand if you look down or away most of the time, you show them lack of confidence. Too much stare at a person will make him feel very much uncomfortable and he will consider it invasive, to say the least, but this doesn't mean that you should break the eye contact. Keep in mind that you need to be relaxed and also keep it steady. Don't look away as it is going to make them uncomfortable.

Our body posture also matters a lot when it comes to influencing others. Solid research has proved that our standing positions, sitting positions and walking postures greatly affect how we make an impact on others. An active and solid posture while someone talks to you is the way to make a mark on the other people. If you are not active and have adopted a passive stance, the other person will be at an advantage. He will have an upper edge during the communication or any business deal you are going to strike.

Gestures are a part of your expression of certain emotions. They tend to accentuate your message to the people. They add emphasis, warmth as well as openness to your style. Gesturing is considered as a cultural behavior. If your gestures are relaxed and carry meaning, they will inject depth or infuse power to your conversation. Another thing that has a great impact on how you influence others is the distance you keep when you are talking to others. If you are sitting or standing closely to a person, it means that you are very intimate to them with respect to the relationship. Here moderation is the key to success. If you come too close to the other people, you may be on your way to offend them, and they will immediately become defensive. This factor depends on different cultures. In the eastern culture, there is a limit of distance between two people while in the western culture, there is no such limit. It also depends on the mood of the other person. In some cases when you get close to the other person, she may consider it a request to cut down the distance and be intimate with you.

The book has educated you how you can be a better influencer for people. It explained what methods you can use to make other people attracted toward you. It depends on different things such as how you have made your first impression and what elements have you chosen for effective communication. You have learnt the key to influence other people. You have learnt several techniques such as reciprocity, pre-giving technique, consistency and many others. You have also learned what social validation is and how social-proof works.

Influencing is about how you carry yourselves and how your portray yourselves. For example, you should express it what you say by your words. Only then there will be sufficient substance in your message. Have you ever seen someone who is speaking loudly and wearing a smile on his face? The combination is hardly a reality. When we are angry, it is expressed from our words and on the face. You should bring yourself in a certain state of mind and then see how your face looks in the mirror. From there you can calculate what expression should be paired up with what kind of words. Now you can think about something and then match your facial expression with it. This book has equipped you with the techniques and methods you need to be a highly influential person.

PART - III

The Art of Small Talk

How to Master the Unwritten Code of Social Skills, Improve Your Charisma, and Little-Known Hacks to Connect with Anyone Effortlessly

JASON MILLER

Introduction

At some point in our lives, we have all been that socially awkward person. And whether you have come to label yourself as an introvert, or you are an extrovert who is struggling to connect with that inner social butterfly, we have to come to that place where we realize that social interaction with our peers is essential for human growth.

That said, many of us find it difficult to interact with humans. There are a lot of explanations for this, but this time around, I encourage you to stop giving in to those explanations and instead take a stand today to become better at conversations. It is going to be a scary journey, especially for those of us who are shy and reclusive, but that doesn't have to define you going forward. In this book, you can learn how to take charge of your social life and find ways to build relationships that will not only empower and sustain you, but they will nourish you in ways that you didn't think was possible.

Approach this book with an open mind. Let go of any preconceived notions you have about why you are the way you are. As I said earlier, you may have come to put a label over yourself, and what this does is to help you cope better with the distance you have with the people in your life. However, as humans, we are biologically programmed to seek out each other. There is a longing on the inside of you. Something that wants you to reach out and connect. This is perfectly normal. In this book, I share with you my journey to becoming an extrovert. Now, I use the label 'extrovert,' not because I am the typical definition of someone who enjoys being in crowds. I am reflecting on how I left the place where it was difficult for me to even establish eye contact to this point where I can meet a complete stranger, smile and start a conversation. These are milestones that I crossed, and while it was hard at first, I can tell you that over time, it got easier.

If you are planning on becoming a public speaker, this will provide the foundation or premise for that journey. In this book, you will also learn how to interact with people in a public setting because public speaking is more than just standing on stage and talking to the crowd. You have to connect with them, and while it is a lot easier to connect with people when you are in a one-on-one setting, it is not impossible to replicate that effect in a group setting. And that is just one of the many things you are going to learn in this book. So, as you flip to the next chapter, take a deep and positive breath, let go of your fears, and what you think you can or cannot do. Make your mind a blank slate because here on out, we are writing new experiences in your social life and we are going to do it in style.

So, turn over and let us begin.

Chapter One: Why is it Hard for You to Talk to People?

Before we start reeling out a three-point solution to the problem at hand, it is important to get to the root of the problem first of all. And to get to the root, we seek to answer the questions of why we are the way we are. The better understanding you have about why you act the way you do, the more effective you become at implementing the solutions. More than that, knowing the root of the problem gives you deeper insight into your personality and helps you make sense of the world around you.

Why is it Scary to Talk to People?

If we are going to look into all the reasons explaining why talking to some people might seem like a scary experiment, we will be here until 12 Sundays from now, and we still would not have exhausted half of those reasons. To save us from that stress, I will focus on just one reason. And that reason is very simple; we project our perception of ourselves on other people. Let me explain that.

When we try to talk to people (and by 'we' here, I am talking about us shy folks), we think of how they would react towards us. Before we meet people, we have a certain image of ourselves when it comes to how we look and how we sound. And often, we feel that these perceptions do not match up to the required social standards. And so every time we meet new people, we feel that they are judging us based on these opinions we have about ourselves. In other words, we think for people when we come across them. And then, on top of that, we insert our negative opinions about ourselves into those thoughts that we are thinking on behalf of those people.

Do you realize how ridiculous that sounds? But that is essentially what we do, and because we think that people are thinking these things about us, it makes it difficult to approach them. These thoughts are not always self-conceived. As in, we do not just sit down and create those thoughts. More often than not, these are things that have happened based on experience. Probably in our childhood, we had a social setting where we were embarrassed by our peers who brutally capitalized on our insecurities. Or perhaps, our parents may have directly or indirectly sowed the seeds of self-doubt in our hearts and we grew up with this unpleasant notion about ourselves.

Another possible root for the negative opinions we have about ourselves could be from the kinds of content that we feed our minds. There are a lot of books, magazines and content out there in the world telling us how we should look. And when we are different from these things, we develop insecurities about those differences. Our fear of talking to people comes from a place of insecurity and to get over it; we would first need to get over ourselves.

Where Does Fear Come From?

Fear is a biological response to anything that threatens your being. When you are afraid, the fear that you experience triggers a survival instinct bent on preserving you. So, if your fear is activated when you get into a social setting, essentially, your mind or brain is trying to preserve you from any perceived dangers in your environment, and this happens because your brain has come to look at social settings as a place that threatens your well-being. This is not something you were born with. It is something that is emphasized over time, like a habit.

Fear is not the horrible monster we have come to know. We may not be like how it makes us feel, but if you look at fear from an objective perspective and get an understanding of it, you would realize that you can harness it for your own good. Fear keeps you alert. Now, when you indulge in fear for too long, you become paranoid. However, if you are able to plug yourself into the root of your fear, you can use that knowledge to empower yourself and what do I mean by this?

Since we now know that fear in social settings is triggered because your mind has been conditioned to think that you are being threatened every time you get into a social situation, you can now work out a process of reprogramming your mind to think the opposite. This is not something that is going to happen overnight, as it would require deliberate effort on your part. However, with the commitment, you can make it happen.

I should point out here that for a small group of us, the fear that we experience when we get into social situations is part of our biological makeup and I cannot fully go into the details of that here. This because it is something that will require collaboration with your doctor if you fall under that spectrum. That said, there are still tips you can pick up from this book along the way. I believe that biological makeup or not, there is a psychological angle to this and that is what we want to tackle in this book.

Mental Barriers to Talking to People

Have you ever been in a situation where you finally walk up the courage to talk to a person only to find yourself paralyzed completely on the spot? Even after you spent days to rehearse your lines and conversations, the moment it gets to that point where you were supposed to step onto the plate, you lose it and have that deer caught in the light situation. It is not pleasant. I can tell you for sure because I have been in that boat and there are a lot of reasons for it. Most of which have to do with fear, but seeing as we have already talked about fear in the previous segment, let us look at other reasons that explain the embarrassing situation.

1. Insecurities

We touched on this area earlier when we first started out this chapter. And we are discussing this here because this is a major contributory factor to the mental barriers we experience in our attempts at social interaction. When we try to initiate conversations with people, we are often focused on who we think we are. To make matters worse, we have negative opinions about who we are and this acts as a block in our ability to talk with people.

2. Assertion of Assumptions

When we meet a person, based on certain poor analysis like how the person dresses, the way they talk and so on, we judge them. And based on this judgement, we react. What we have done here is basically to assert an assumption that we have about the person. This causes conflict in conversations because we are unable to get past this mental opinion that we have generated about this person. There is a common phrase that says," do not judge a book by its cover." Many of us take a look at the external attributes of a person without really looking inward to know a person. And without that insight, it is going to be impossible to have a genuine conversation with said person.

3. Language

Language is one of the most complex aspects of human communication. And here, I am looking beyond the differences in our mother and focusing on our perception of what is said and being said to us. Words connote different meanings to each of us and for this reason, we develop different reactions to certain words and phrases. This would explain why certain phases that may have caused a certain group of people to laugh might cause another person to cry. These differences in language can make it difficult for us to talk to people, especially when you consider the fact that shy people are typically very sensitive.

Now that we have set up a premise for why we find it difficult to talk to people, the next course of action is to look into the fears that we face every time we get into a social setting and explore effective ways to overcome it.

Chapter Two: The Foundation of Social Anxiety and Learning to Cope

Social anxiety happens when a person develops a fear of being rejected, judged or negatively evaluated and this feeling of fear is usually brought on or triggered by being in a social setting. The manifestation of social anxiety is usually in one's performance, so in a roundabout way, you can say that social anxiety is performance issues triggered by fear from being in a social setting. If any of this sounds like something you can relate with, you are not alone. Millions of people all over the world suffer from some form of social anxiety or the other. In the next few segments, we will explore the topic in detail and come up with tips on how to maintain high performance even when you are under social pressure due to anxiety.

How to Overcome Social Anxiety

The impact that social anxiety has on our lives is tremendous. However, it does not mean that it cannot be overcome. There are measures you can put in place to help you with the daily steps needed to overcome social anxiety and a lot of these steps are things that you can start doing from your home. That said, it is important to know what spectrum you fall under when it comes to diagnosing a social anxiety disorder. It is a well-known fact that people who suffer from severe and extreme cases would need to rely on drugs and therapy to overcome their struggles. Outside that, these next few steps that I am going to talk about are things that are basically doable from where you are right. If you have already spoken to your doctor, go ahead and put the steps to practice. Build on it and through it; you can build your esteem enough to help you overcome social anxiety.

1. Confront the situation that triggers your anxiety head-on

It is human to want to immediately take yourself outside situations that cause you to feel a certain kind of way about yourself. However, if you are serious about overcoming anxiety, it is important that you put yourself out there. Just ensure that you do this in moderate and controlled doses. Don't plan on going from being a couch buddy to a cliff jumping adventurer in minutes.

2. Keep a journal

An emotional journal is there to help you keep track of your feelings. That way, you can narrow down the specific emotions that trigger your anxiety. It could be fear, anger or sometimes it could just be activities that take you down memory lane to a negative experience that you had in the past. Knowing your triggers will help you become better prepared

3. Get physical

Physical exercise has a way of making us feel good and better about our bodies, not to mention the fact that it helps you explore your mental headspace and gets you into a positive mindset faster.

4. Let go of any illusions you have about being perfect

Most people who suffer from social anxiety disorder have a problem with performance in public. And that is because they think that people expect them to be perfect. It is impossible to be perfect. Let go of the desire to get people to see you as perfect. It is okay to be you the way you are.

5. Stay positive

Being positive is an essential part of your journey to overcoming social anxiety. Train yourself to stop wandering to the dark and negative recesses of your mind. Focus instead on those things that make you feel good about you as a person and the life that you live.

Advantages of Learning Techniques and Education on Social Skills

Essentially, social skills help to prep you for easy integration into social settings that you are not familiar with. It could be for business purposes or a simple education on how to do certain things when you are in public with people. These things that I am talking about are basically what people consider as proper social skills and it can range from basic conversation to traditionally acceptable interaction based on a specific geography. It is important to learn the skills so that you do not end up offending people.

Beyond that, being knowledgeable of common social skills makes it easier to communicate, as certain social faux pas that may be regarded as disrespectful can quickly earn you the tag of rude or difficult to associate with. And when you have these kinds of tags in social settings, you might as well be wearing the scarlet letter on your forehead. People tend to avoid those that are wearing such tags.

In life, you never know how far you are going to go. You cannot always judge your progression in life based on the people you are associating with you right now. It is possible that in the course of your business or career progression, you could find yourself in some of the most amazing cities and places in the world. Beyond the language barrier which could prevent communication, there are also other things that make interaction in these kinds of settings, and having good knowledge of the social skills tell are peculiar to that region can help you understand what is acceptable and proper.

The Case for Learning About Confidence and Social Skills Together

Knowing the importance of social skills is one thing. Implementing them is another and this is where confidence comes in. A person who is confident in their ability and personality does not let that get in the way of them using the knowledge that they have gained to their advantage. Whether they are in the boardrooms negotiating the next big deal or they are pitching their brands and ideas to potential investors ... or perhaps it's a child speaking up for the first time. Whatever category you fall under, confidence is the key to executing the social skills you have gained in real life.

One way you can go about boosting your confidence is by getting rid of the notion that you are not good enough. I had a counselor who used to tell me that, "if you don't love yourself, how can you expect other people to love you in the same way." It is important to build self-care routines as well as indulge in treats every now and then to help you climb out of that hole of insecurities and self-doubt. You need to begin to take on activities that affirm the many skills that you have to reveal the true personality within and discover people who share the same interests with you. In the next chapter, we will go into more detail about confidence and how to build it. This segment is meant to set a premise for confidence and how it plays out and social interaction.

The combination of being confident and having an understanding of how people interact in a certain setting has a way of portraying us as the ideal person that people should relate with. When people have this kind of perception about you, your social life will experience a massive boost and in my opinion, this is a win-win situation for everyone involved.

Chapter Three: Building Confidence for Better Social Interaction

Confidence, as we have discussed previously, is an essential ingredient for any social interaction; whether you are talking to one single person or a group of three, the right amount of confidence can set the tone for that relationship. You may have heard people use the term "doormats." This usually refers to people who are unable to assert themselves in their relationships and this inability finds its root cause is a lack of confidence. Without confidence, you will not be able to express yourself articulately. And when you are unable to express yourself articulately, people who you are in a relationship with tend to overlook your needs. So, it is important to build one's confidence.

Where Does Confidence Come From?

To put it in very short and simple terms, confidence comes from your own perception of yourself and abilities. In other words, the image or concept you have about yourself is what feeds your confidence. If you have a very poor opinion of yourself, there is a very strong possibility that you will not be a confident person. Confidence has been linked to self-esteem issues and that explains why people with poor self-esteem tend to have poor confidence.

However, while confidence is an innate ability, I would say that the society around you can influence the level of confidence that you have. So if you have people or are surrounded by people who constantly affirm your negative opinion of yourself, this would reduce your self-esteem and in doing so, reduce your confidence. The opposite happens when you surround yourself with people who affirm the positive opinion that you have about yourself. Your confidence level will soar and you find yourself doing amazing things.

Now, some people find it easier to develop confidence. You would find children who are born confident and then you have kids who find it difficult even to maintain eye contact with their peers. Over time, the society that grooms them (which includes their family, their friends, their network at school and outside the school and so on) can determine how far the confidence level of this child goes. That said, if you are struggling with confidence, the first step to building it recognizes that you are more than the opinion that you have about yourself.

The Basic Foundation for Growing the Confidence You Need

The most common tip you get when it comes to building your confidence would be to 'fake it until you make it.' Now, this can come in handy in certain situations. However, it is important to understand that there is a fine line between confidence and arrogance. And if you are faking it, your confidence can sometimes come off as arrogance. Genuine confidence has very little to do with pride or looking down on other people. As I established earlier, confidence is all about who you feel you are on the inside and not about the people on the outside.

If you are constantly putting yourself up against the people in your environment and using that as a yardstick to measure yourself with, you have crossed the line of being confident and entered into arrogance territory. That said, here are some tips on how to grow your confidence;

1. Avoid negative places and people

Nothing pulls your confidence down faster than surrounding yourself with people who are constantly negative. Take yourself out of that environment and find a space that will nurture you positively.

2. Do not accept other people's negative opinion of you

People's notions about you may have been fed by some error or mistake you made in the past but that does not essentially define you. If they insist on identifying you with that negative trait or history, that is their problem. You, on the other hand, do not need to deal with their inability to move past that point.

3. Find your voice

For me, I think that this is the most critical part of developing your confidence. You need to find what is important to you and learn how to voice those needs. You may not have to put it into words right away, but acknowledging to yourself the things that are important to you is a great start.

4. Have a strong support system

Whether it is your family, mentor, or basically people who you often get a positive vibe off, it is important that you build your own village or community of cheerleaders. These are people who genuinely care about your well-being and see the potential that you have on the inside.

Asserting Your Confidence in Social Situations

Before going further in this book, I would like you to ask yourself the following questions; what does confidence look like for you in a social situation? Are you one of those people who feel that talking down or ensuring that your voice is the loudest makes you the most confident? If so, it is time to change that mentality. Confidence is more than just how you appear, although, that also plays a role. However, I feel that appearance and confidence basically stem from being comfortable in outfits that you wear.

A lot of people tend to focus on what they wear (in terms of the designer brand), as well as social status. They also tend to lean on their wealthy background or rich educational history like a confidence crutch of some sort. All this is well and good, but they don't necessarily help your standing when it comes to confidence in a social setting. They may open doors for you, but they will certainly not keep you in the room. Confidence in the social setting is basically learning to speak and while speaking is an essential part of expressing your confidence, listening is just as important. When you feel to listen to people, communication automatically shuts down.

It is for this reason that I firmly believe that in social settings, confidence is a juggling act between speaking and listening at the right and opportune time. Confidence in communication also extends beyond the verbal aspect. You can use your body language to communicate and confidence can be expressed in your body language. For instance, slouching your shoulders is considered a sign of poor confidence. Also, one's inability to maintain eye contact can be interpreted as poor confidence. And here is my final tip. When next you are given a handshake, ensure that the handshake is firm. That is a nonverbal display of confidence. These tiny attributes are the things that make up what confidence looks like in social interactions.

Chapter Four: Understanding the Mechanics of Human Interaction

Humans are biologically programmed to seek out each other's company. No matter how much of a loner you claim to be, at the end of the day, there is an unspoken need and desire to connect with other people. This desire is the foundation of human interaction. However, there are laws and rules that guide this process. These laws are not what you find in the constitution. What you should expect to find is the fact that there are socially acceptable behaviors that come to play when you are looking at human interaction. Beyond social skills and etiquette, this chapter was going to go in-depth on how this process works and you get some tips on playing this knowledge to your advantage.

The Basic Psychological Principles of Human Interaction

This segment is meant to focus on why we interact with each other as humans. By understanding the purpose of human interaction and the psychology that guides that process, we better equip ourselves with the right tools (or mindset if you prefer) that will get us to where we want socially.

The very first basic psychological principle of human interaction is the fact that every social relationship that we have serves a goal. Now, that goal may have been plotted out consciously and deliberately. Or sometimes, it is just something that we gravitate to naturally because it suits a need. In a situation where social interaction is deliberate, the person who makes a conscious effort to interact with specific people does it usually to meet a transactional need. For instance, the person may feel that by interacting with this particular individual, they may be able to get the opportunities that would lead to their growth in a work environment or their social status.

This is not to say that the person does it with malicious intent. This person simply sees social interaction as a means to an end. Now let us look at the flip side to this. On an unconscious level, you have this person who gravitates towards a person socially to meet some form of emotional need. This is very common with us, especially if we grew up lacking a parental figure or what we term as an ideal role model in our lives. We try to fill up that hole in our lives with the people that we meet and the relationships that we build with them. When we meet someone who we feel matches the profile of our expectations, we use the relationship that we have with them to replace our losses.

Going forward, it is important to understand why you are entering into relationships with people. And while you are on the subject, try to figure out why these people that you meet might be trying to establish relationships with you. Is it for emotional reasons or transactional reasons? The goal does not necessarily have to determine your acceptance of that relationship. It simply helps you understand where you stand with that person and how to proceed in terms of communication and all of the other topics we have addressed in the previous chapters.

Difference in Manipulation Vs Influence Based on True Connection, Intimacy and Serving Others

Given everything we have talked about so far, it is understandable if you start using the words, influence, and manipulations interchangeably. However, these words have two very distinct meanings and their application in relationships have the ability to break or build that relationship. It is therefore important to understand the differences between these two words. Because, if you take everything that you learn in this book and decide to use it to your advantage without really understanding the concept behind it, you would find that rather than building good and healthy relationships you have set the tone for manipulations and nobody likes to be manipulated.

Manipulations may yield you the results that you want temporarily, but it could go on to destroy whatever future that relationship had. Influence or the other hand, can impact the choices and decisions that the other person in the relationship with you makes. But, if you are coming from a place of genuine connection and intimacy, it has the ability to enhance communication and promote room for healthy growth. Manipulations involve the use of sinister and devious practices to get your way such practices could include lying, blackmail and threats masked as requests. Other forms of manipulations involve degrading a person to a point where they start to question their own opinions as well as the manipulation of elements in the environment to simulate control.

Influence, on the other hand, employs techniques such as concession, which is basically what happens during negotiation. It also uses authority so people in a position of authority can influence the people that they are leading. Another key principle of influence that a lot of us use is the simple act of 'likeness'. If you like a person, there is a very big possibility that you would go the extra mile for that person and a lot of us use this to our advantage. In this situation, the lines between manipulation and Influence might become blurred, but it tilts more towards influence because your emotions towards that person influence your decisions.

Basic Ideas of What People Think in a Conversation and Social Interactions

If you have ever sat down during a conversation and thought to yourself, "what is this person thinking?", you are not alone. Beyond the subject matter of the conversation that we have with people, there is this innate curiosity that makes us wonder what our conversation mates are thinking. While it is impossible to decode those thoughts at the moment (given the fact that we have no mind reader), there are certain things that can clue us into the mindset of the person. I am not going to go into the specifics when it comes to the thoughts because, different strokes for different folks, as they say. However, I am going to go into some of the different things that can influence the thoughts of a person in social settings.

The Environment

The setting where you find yourself in plays a major role in what the person might be thinking about. For instance, if you are in a work environment, the line of thought would have to relate to the performance issues or anxieties about the performance issues. That is not to say that people in these environments do not think about anything outside the place of work. But this is in line with what is generally acceptable.

The Roles that They Play

The roles that people play influences what they think about in conversations or social interactions. For instance or parents would think more in the lines of things that affect the ability to parent as well as what impacts the future of their wards or children. So, if you find yourself in a conversation with a parent to enhance the conversation, you may want to find common ground by looking at their roles as parents. It is common knowledge that many parents are very proud of their children and the moment you strike up a conversation about their kids, it is always difficult to get them to stop (just kidding).

Their Emotional State

Around Valentine's season, cakes, cards, and flower vendors experience a spike in sales and when you look into their customer base, you find out that a lot of people who buy their products are couples or people who are intending to go into relationships. This speaks to the emotional state of people during that season. My point is, when striking up conversations with people, if you decode their emotional state accurately, you may be able to key into their thoughts and establish a connection with them. During Valentine, this is what these vendors tap into to make their sales pitch.

Chapter Five: The Art of Small Talk

I think the biggest mistake a lot of people make is to assume that small talk is basically those pointless words that you use in an attempt to keep the conversation going. They failed to realize that small talk is the actual engine that drives a conversation. It may feel awkward initially, especially if you are not in an informal relationship with that person. However, if you do it right regardless of whatever phase that relationship is in, you can build a foundation that leads to death if it is what you desire. Whatever your relationship goals are, the fact remains that with small talk you can set the tone for the direction in the area of communication.

The Goal of Small Talk in Conversations

There are several reasons people use small talk in conversations and I will be going into some of them. However, just as I said in the introduction, small talk is a very important engine that is useful in driving a conversation. That said, let us look at the goals of small talk and perhaps, this will help you understand just how important it is.

1. It establishes a connection

Small talk typically evolves around relatable topics and with those kinds of topics, you can use it to get a feel of how the person you are communicating with sees the world without really getting in-depth. This is particularly useful if you are not familiar with the person in the first place. With small talk, you can get to know the person without making an awkward situation even more awkward.

2. It is a coping mechanism for people with anxiety

Social anxiety is more common than you think and we know that it happens when you find yourself in a social setting. If you are trying to break out of your shell and get into that place where communicating with people is no longer tedious, one of the first things you would have to learn how to do is small talk. Small talk is an excellent defense mechanism as it helps you participate in the conversation without dreading the outcome of it and this is because the conversation you are having is in shallow waters, so to speak and offers you safety.

3. It opens up a window for dialogue

This comes in very handy if you are at a networking event and you are trying to get to know people. Rather than coming outright and blurting out your credentials without really getting to know the person, inserting a little small talk into the conversation can set the premise for how the rest of your communication with that person will turn out. If you are able to do the small talk right, the person you are having a conversation with would be more open to hearing the rest of what you actually intend to say.

These three that I have just listed here are particularly useful for the objective that we have in terms of mastering the art of communication. The small talk goes beyond having to discuss the weather and in a few short moments, you are going to learn more on the subject. Just bear in mind that regardless of your personality type, small talk is essential for conversations to thrive.

Conversation Flow

If I wanted to give this topic a definition, I would say that conversation flow essentially is the smooth transition from one topic to another. When you are having an extensive conversation with a person, if you stay on one topic for too long, it might get boring. And if the topic is a sensational one, tempers might flare-up. So, it is important that you consciously apply effort in ensuring that the conversation moves freely from one topic to another. Now, in a bid to stir up the conversation flow, it is also important that you don't just jump from one topic to another. Because then, you start to look like you are unsure of what you are doing. In this segment, I am going to guide you on how to establish a healthy conversation flow even with a stranger.

Step one: Create a doorway for the conversation

A doorway is the starting point for any conversation. Whether you are in an informal setting or any place where everyone is professional, you need a doorway to get you into a conversation. Now informal settings, a lot of people tend to go with the introduction route. They start a conversation by introducing themselves. That works too, but the most effective way to get the attention of a person you want to talk to in a formal setting is to bring the focus on them. What do I mean by that? Say you are aware of what the person does for a living, you can latch onto that as the introduction. An example of being, "Hi, I overheard that you are a software engineer. Do you work primarily with websites or applications?".

A question like that will force them to respond but there's also a great chance that they would respond happily because this is a subject that they are interested in. On the other hand, if you find yourself in an informal setting, a great way to stir up a conversation is by asking questions. However, ensure that the question you are asking is not a 'yes or no' kind of question. It should be a question that will cause them to be involved in their response. An example would be, "Hi there, I am very new at all this and you look like someone who is very much at home here. So, I was wondering if you could make a recommendation for me". Again this puts the person at the forefront of the conversation. If you ask politely and keep your demeanor pleasant, you might be able to start up a conversation.

The choice of the way for the conversation should be dependent on the situation you find yourself in. If you are on a date or an interview, or perhaps you are meeting up with investors, the doorway for the conversation must match the situation.

Step two: Initiate small talk

This is the part that some people have trouble with. But if you pay attention closely, I would say that this is the easiest part. The main ingredient for initiating good small talk is listening. Now, if you end up with a person who is not really into conversations, you may have to do more of the talking, but listen to their responses as well because their responses will cue you in on what the next topic of conversation should be. For example, if you meet the person in a museum and you were able to create a doorway for conversation, rather than ask them about when they developed their passion for art, focus on the little details that they offer you. For instance, if they mention the name of a particular artist, let that be a conversation lead. Make a comparison with the artist that they mentioned with another artist and get their opinions on it.

This is small talk, but in a way, it is helping you get to know the person. So, create the doorway then listen to their responses. Pick up on topics that you are knowledgeable about and find that they are also interested in to initiate the next topic of conversation. It is also fine if you allow the other person to lead you into the next topic. Avoid being monotonous in your responses. Giving yes or no answers when you are having a small talk is a big conversation killer. So, endeavor to respond in three to four sentences and perhaps ask a few questions of your own. As you ask your questions, try not to sound as though you are interrogating the person because that makes people defensive. Instead, affirm their choices and if you don't agree with them on certain topics, politely express your view without using it as an opportunity to convert them.

Step three: Time your conversation

If you keep the conversation short and sweet, people are more likely going to remember you. However, if you continue droning on about subjects that you find fascinating, there is a very big possibility that if that same person sees you at another event, they will avoid you. Especially if they don't share the same interests with you. So, when you get into conversations with people it is important that you time it in such a way that you are able to exit the conversation when the excitement is still high. There is a proverb that says, "leave when the applause is at its loudest." This applies to conversations as well. In a bid to keep your conversation short, I do not encourage you to be checking your time because of that in its own way as rude. However, there are body signs given by your partner in conversation that you can use to decide if it is time to exit that conversation.

For example, if you start noticing that the person you are talking to is glancing about the room, that is a sign that they are looking for someone else to talk to. At this point in time, this is your cue to step back. Another important cue to look out for is if they are checking their own time. These subtle body languages are informing you that the conversation has come to an end. However, if you find that the conversation is riveting with both of you being reluctant to end it, I would still say that for a first meeting, especially if you are in a formal setting where the goal is networking, you should try to end the conversation. That said when you end the conversation with someone like this, ensure that you take their contact details as this could lead to more conversations or communications in the future. But as of the moment, your focus in this setting is to network and you want to mingle and meet up with as many people as possible.

If you are going to stick to time, then I will say in a formal setting, 5 minutes is a lot to spend with one person. That should not mean you end the conversation abruptly. You listen to what they have to say, express your fascination with their ideas and then inform them that you were pleased to meet them; however, it is time for you to move on. Exchange cards where possible and exit the conversation politely.

5 Principles For Success In Conversations

Given everything we have learned so far from the art of small talk to ensure that you have a smooth and healthy conversation flow, this segment is going to break down the guiding principles of a successful conversation. This will go on to help you identify those elements that make the conversation interesting, relatable and most importantly guarantees a repeat;

1. You are good with descriptions

In the mouth of a good conversationalist, words are like the paintbrush in the hand of a painter. The words that you use help to paint a mental picture and that picture is what your conversation partner would identify with. Your inability to use words to describe or articulate your thoughts is the reason why people have miscommunications. Because the words paint a different picture from the message that is being passed across. This is something that you are going to have to learn and groom yourself in.

2. Creative use of contrasts and comparisons

When having conversations, the comparisons and contrasts that you use have a way of enriching the image that you create. For example, instead of just saying that the beauty (of a person or thing you are describing) is delicate, you go on to say the beauty of that person is as delicate as a rose flower. What you have done there is to make the picture you are painting richer and all the more interesting. Comparisons that you use enhances the richness of a conversation.

3. The use of body language

The use of body language in a conversation is essential for the success of that conversation. Whether you like it or not, subconsciously, you are sending out messages with your body. Now, if you make a deliberate effort to ensure that the gestures you make and the facial expressions that you have matches the tempo of your conversation, you sound more interesting. And the reason for that is, your body language animates the conversation.

4. Voice inflection

Excitement can be infectious and the reason for this has been linked to the way we express our excitement. Apart from our non-verbal communication, which includes body language and facial expression, there is also our voice inflection. Have you noticed that when you are excited, your voice pitch takes on a different note? The ability to control your voice inflection is the reason why a lot of radio personalities able to drive interesting conversations over the radio even though you are not actively involved in that communication. When your voice pitch takes on a single monotonous pattern, you become bored quickly. That kind of speech pattern is best reserved for bedtime routines for children as it has the ability to induce sleep. During conversations, you want to keep it interesting so, learn to fluctuate in your voice pitch.

Just remember that when you go too high, you sound crazy and when you get too low, you sound weird. Keep your pitch range somewhere in the middle.

5. *Interesting topics*

When you are having conversations with people, the topic focus should not just be a subject that you find interesting. Your partner in the conversation has to find that topic interesting too. That way, both your interests intersect. You may be one of those people who can talk about the incubation period of the caterpillar and find it so fascinating. However, not everybody is interested in the sordid details surrounding this phenomenon. So, as I mentioned in the previous segment, pick up cues as to what both of you find interesting and elaborate on that. If you apply all of the four previously mentioned principles of a successful conversation, it is bound to make the topic even more engaging.

Having laid out these five basic principles, I feel like I should point out here that no conversation can truly become successful if you fail to listen to your conversation partner. The cues for your conversation guide will come from the details obtained when you listen to that person. You may enjoy the sound of your voice and you may have some interesting contributions to make to that conversation; however, you must remember that conversation is not entirely about you and therefore, you need to give room for the other person to share their thoughts and opinions.

Chapter Six: How to Initiate Non-Verbal Communication

Before you open your mouth to speak, there are ways that your body can communicate. The information that you put out there with your body even though it is subconscious could go a long way in helping other people around you form an opinion about you. For instance, if you are in a public space and you are standing with your arms crossed across your chest, people immediately get the way that you do not want to have a conversation. And even though this is not your intention, your body language is saying you are a no-go area. So, this chapter is about helping you learn how to be more deliberate in the way you communicate without saying a word.

How to Smile

A smile is an involuntary response to something that makes you happy or brings you joy. There are a lot of scientific studies that have been conducted on the benefits of a smile and the results of these studies have linked smiles with longevity, health as well as attractiveness. It is said that smiling makes you more physically attractive and not just to yourself but to the people around you. Now, this attraction is not just about physical beauty. What this means here is that a smile can act as a social magnet that attracts people to you. When you smile in a public space, essentially, you are speaking non-verbally and telling the people around you that you are approachable and available for a conversation.

I did say that as well as an involuntary response; however, it doesn't mean that you can only smile when you feel happy or see something that gives you joy. You can deliberately initiate a smile even though you are not experiencing any of these emotions I mentioned. When I was younger, my mother was very fond of saying this, "fake it until you make it," and she was talking about my smile. I wasn't much of the smiler and anytime we went out, she was constantly encouraging me to smile. At first, when I curve my lips upwards in an attempt to smile, I felt ridiculous and somewhat embarrassed. But I found that as the seconds progressed, I genuinely started feeling like I needed to smile. Going by my experience, of course, in that first stage, the smile can seem painful. If you have ever witnessed a painful smile, you know what I mean... that one where your teeth are grinding against each other and the muscles on the side of your face become strained from the effort you are putting into a smile. That, in my opinion, is not a smile. It is a grimace.

The key to faking a smile is keeping it as natural as possible. And since we already know that a smile is an involuntary reaction to something that gives you joy, we start by focusing on elements around you that make you happy. It could be the color used in the decoration; it could be the snacks that were served, or you could focus on people that you actually like. If the atmosphere around you does not appeal to you in any way, then you could focus internally. Draw on images that make you smile; it could be an old joke or the thought of engaging in an activity that you enjoy. Let these pleasant memories motivate your smile. Now when you do smile, try not to display all of your dentition at once because then you look ridiculous and scary. A small but genuine smile is all it takes to get the wagon rolling.

How to use your eyes/body language

In romantic folklore, they say that the eyes are the windows to the soul. I don't know how true that is, but I do know this; if you do not channel your gaze properly, you can come across as one of many things and one of those things could be the vibe that you are an unpleasant person to be around. When you step into a new environment and you find yourself glancing around, people read you as someone who is nervous and with something to hide. If you decide to glare at people every time they look at you, the interpretation they will get is that you are a person with malicious intent. This also happens when it comes to body language. If your arms or legs are crossed, whether you are standing or sitting, it reads as though you are turning people away. The message that they get from you, essentially, is that you are not available for conversation.

Even if you are not having a one-on-one conversation with people, if you find yourself in a position where you are on a stage talking to a crowd of people, your body language can either support the words you are saying or contradict them. You can use your eyes to express interest in a person or express your disgust of their person. Your eyes can also make a person feel intimidated by your presence, or you can help that person feel as though they are welcome into your space. The language of the eyes and the body is one of the most basic forms of communication. When you were born, you did not have the gift of garb, yet somehow, your parents can read your expression and understand that you have certain feelings about certain things… even though you never expressly stated those emotions. As we grow into languages and understand how to communicate without words, our eyes and our bodies still have an essential message to pass across.

More often than not, I believe that our bodies have a way of communicating the true intent of our hearts. Even if your words are saying one thing, people are paying attention to the way your hands are moving and to the expressions on your face. I remember a hilarious incident that happened when I was much younger. My younger sister was being introduced to lime. We talked about the lime; about how sharp and bitter, the taste was. But this particular brother of mine was bragging about how he loved the taste of lime and so, my mother bought lime for him that day. He tasted it and of course, immediately, he was hit with the sharp sensations and although the words that came out from his mouth were, "I love it," we saw his facial expression and it told us everything we needed to know. His eyes were squeezed shot which basically told us that he could not stand the taste and his face was scrunched up in a way that further emphasized what the eyes were already telling us.

Our body language and our expressions during conversation may not be as intense as my brother's lime lying experiment, however, for people who pay attention to your body language, they get the true message just as clearly as we did.

How to Come Across and Credible and Confident Without Words

Even for the most social person, I would say that it is not every time they walk into a room full of people that they immediately feel confident. They are simply just better adept at masking their emotions. In this segment, we are going to focus on those non-verbal ways to communicate your confidence even before you say a single word. There are several books that focus on this subject because of the volume of information available on this. However, I am going to keep it short and simple by focusing on the basics. As you continue to practice your conversation skills, you would evolve and grow this list.

1. Dress the part

The dressing has a way of building your confidence, and when you look confident, you feel confident. If you are invited to an event, endeavor to put work towards ensuring that the clothes you wear to the event match the theme. That way, you do not stand out as the oddball. One thing I would like you to take note of here is that dressing the part does not mean you have to spend a lot of money on your clothing or wear designer gear. There are three things you need to focus on when it comes to dressing the part. One is your comfort, two is your style and then three is the fit of the outfit.

Comfort does not necessarily mean you have to wear slacks and bunny slippers. Comfort is ensuring that you are able to move around comfortably in that outfit without feeling as though your dressing is going to fall apart. It also means prioritizing what makes you feel comfortable over what is fashionable. So, a nice pair of flats may be more comfortable for you than a six-inch heel. The heels are very attractive and fashionable, but you risk falling down and injuring yourself. It is better to stick with sensible shoes. Choose a pair that are formal. The next part is your style. If you are not into high fashion drama, there is no need to get into the latest trends. Stick to what you genuinely enjoy. When it comes to style, again, all you need to keep in mind is ensuring that your personal style is in tandem with the theme for the event you are attending.

Finally, ensure that the clothes you are wearing are fitted. When clothes match your body size perfectly, it enhances your strengths and hides your flaws, making you look exceptionally beautiful or handsome, as the case may be. This goes on to provide you with confidence.

2. Maintain a good posture

Slouched shoulders, hunched back and a low-hanging chin are classic indicators of poor confidence and low self-esteem issues. So it is important that you maintain a good posture. Stand upright, keep your head held up high and avoid slouching your shoulders. The key to attaining the perfect posture is just like attaining a natural smile. You have to try to keep your posture as natural as possible so that you don't come off looking stiff. Because, if you look stiff, the message you are passing across to people who might be coming your way is that you are someone who is not fun and we both know that you are an amazing person for people to know. All you have to do is give them a chance. It starts by keeping the doors open. What do I mean? Ensure that your posture says you are welcoming, inviting and accessible.

3. Don't run away from direct contact

When you meet someone, you instinctively reach out your hand for a handshake. This is a ritual in communication that must be adhered to. When you are in a handshake, ensure that your grip is firm. However, don't make it too firm that you hurt the person. Another thing you have to try to do is to maintain eye contact. Averting your gaze when there is a contact might be interpreted as you being either shy or lacking when it comes to confidence. A confident person is able to hold another person's gaze. If you feel that it is too tedious to maintain eye contact with a person, try this simple trick I learned. Gaze at the person for 10 seconds, then look away to a distance that is no longer than 10 feet away from you for another 10 seconds before returning your gaze to the person. This way, you don't have to feel intimidated by that process. You engage the person with your eyes, take your gaze away for a few seconds and then return the focus to that person. In a more intimate setting, I would advise that you hold that gaze for longer. It builds the connection you have with that person.

Chapter Seven: Becoming a Master at Small Talk

Small talk is the engine that drives a conversation which eventually leads to building lasting relationships. If you are able to master the art of small talk, you will become an excellent conversationalist. People love to talk with someone who has something interesting to say. But more importantly, they also want to be heard. Small talk is not just about you talking.

It is about creating an atmosphere that allows for easy communication and communication can only happen if you allow the other person to have room to express their opinions. And just so you know, the subject of the small talk does not really matter as long as you are able to handle it delicately.

You could be discussing the weather and still make it such a fascinating subject that the other person involved becomes engaged. This is what it means to master small talk.

How to Start Small Talk

Knowing what we know now about small talk, here are a few pointers to help you get started;

Step one: Put your phone aside

Small talk is not the time to start showing off the make and model of your phone or trying to view the latest happening on Instagram. Social media has made it possible for us to connect with people all over the world; however, because of the numerous voices on the platform, it has made us more disconnected from our real world. I watched a movie once where this nice family was having dinner. And the whole room was quiet, not because the food was super delicious, but because everyone was on their phone. A platform where the family was supposed to connect with each other gave room for a total disconnect because of phones. So it is important that you disconnect from social media and your phone in order to connect with the person in front of you.

Step two: Ask open-ended questions

I talked about this earlier, but I didn't go into detail because I knew that we were going to run into this here. The questions that you ask will elicit a response from the person that you are talking to. If you ask simple 'yes or no' type of questions, that is exactly what you would get. You need to learn to ask the type of questions that would require the person responding to use more than two sentences.

Step three: Be enthusiastic

Remember what I said about voice inflections earlier. When you inject excitement into your words, it automatically triggers excitement in the other person. This is because, as humans, we are empathetic by nature and one of the ways we show empathy is by mirroring the action or response of the other person in conversation. Your enthusiasm can become contagious simply because the person empathizes with where you are coming from and they are now mirroring your reaction. It may feel a little fake initially, but the more you practice, the better you become at being excited about the topic of your small talk

Step four: Listen attentively

One thing I have always said in this book is that the foundation for your small talk is basically in the answers that you receive. When you ask those open-ended questions, the responses that you get are what will build the topic for the next set of questions and that is essentially how your conversation will grow. So, pay attention. Besides, you never can tell when the other person would ask a question of their own and if you weren't paying attention or listening to anything they were saying, you might end up making yourself and the person look like a fool.

Step five: Choose your small talk topics carefully

Small talk is not a time to express your political and religious views. Not only is there a very strong possibility that you might end up offending the person you are having a conversation with, but it also creates room for animosity and can make the person that you are having this conversation with feel defensive. When people are defensive, their guards are thrown up, leaving you on the outside. Safe topics for conversation include arts, sports, hobbies, professional interests and of course, my personal favorite, climate.

How To use the FORD Method For Small Talk

The last segment rounded off with the instruction to be careful about the choice of topics for your small talk. There I listed a few examples; however, the Ford method is one of the most reliable ways to decide on the preferred topic for small talk, especially if you are having a conversation with a complete stranger. The Ford method essentially focuses on the acronym FORD, and it means;

F = Family

O = Occupation

R = Recreation

D = Dreams

These are the safest topics to go for when initiating small talk with new people. One thing you should bear in mind, though, is the fact that people react differently to certain questions. This is because they all have their own personal experiences and those experiences are not always pleasant. For instance, a person who is not in very good standing with their family may not be too excited about talking on that subject. It is now left for you to take cues from what they say as well as their body language. The second you get that standoffish or defensive vibe from them, that is your cue to drop the subject. Do not proceed if you sense that the person you are trying to have a conversation with is not comfortable with the choice of topic. That will only ruin things for you and them.

How to Ask Excellent Questions

You would not believe the amount of diplomacy that is required in sustaining a healthy conversation even if you are just meeting that person for the first time. The reason for this diplomacy is that we live in a very sensitive world and people are now beginning to discover and leave their personal truths. Your opinions no longer govern the lives of other people. Now, I am not saying that it did back in the day. It's just that people were more tolerant of outside opinions. Not to mention the fact that they were very into ensuring that their lives were pleasing to those around them.

But all of that is rapidly changing and for this reason, you have to apply caution when you ask certain questions. Even if you are genuinely curious about what is going on in that person's life and you are certain that you have no ulterior motive, you need to respect the boundaries that people have put up and unless you are invited, certain doors on certain subjects will always remain shut. This segment is about helping you find a way to ask those open-ended questions that will not offend or cause the person you are asking those questions to feel insulted. See what I mean about being diplomatic? Anyways, let us get into it.

As I mentioned earlier and open-ended question is basically the kind of question that would require the person in the conversation that has been asked to respond in more than one sentence because it would require them to use their own knowledge and feelings an example of an open-ended question is, " what have you been up to today?". You see that there is no way a person can answer yes or no to that question, they would have to break down how their day went even if they may prefer to give the paraphrased version.

Typically, open-ended questions begin with any of the following words; why, what, describe and explain. The last two words on the list are not really questionnaires on their own; however, they can be used to elicit a lengthy response from the person you are conversing with. If your questions begin with a will, do, are, and so on, the response you are going to get is going to either be a yes or a no with little to no explanation.

The Power of Listening

There are several definitions of the word, listening. However, I would say that the one that most appeals to me is this one that says, "listening is the mindful act of hearing and making an attempt to comprehend what is being said by the other person." In other words, listening is not just hearing the words that being said to you. It is a choice that you have to make to understand what is being said to you. These days a lot of people feel that communication means talking and because we all have something to say, we feel that it must be said. And in our bid to ensure that what we have to say comes out, we fail to pay attention to the words that are coming out from the mouths of the people around us.

Active listening I am told is an essential communication skill. You cannot call yourself a great conversationalist if you fail in the area of listening. What that says about your person is that you are only concerned about your voice as well as the voice in your head. Every other person's opinion might as well be dust; you receive it, but you never make use of it. No matter how smooth you are when it comes to the gift of garb, if you are not a listener, you will not be able to engage your audience. Even in shows where you have comedians on stage doing their bit, despite the fact that the only person doing the talking is the comedian, he or she still listens to the audience for cues and it is those cues that help him deliver his performance exquisitely well.

We have already established that there is both verbal and nonverbal communication. For conversations to go smoothly, you have to pay attention to both what is being said and the body language you are getting from the person. In a situation where you have multiple people talking at once, there is very little possibility of the cause of the problem being resolved and that's because everyone is talking at the same time. The solution will only arise when one person decides to listen and hear the other party out. Mastering the art of small talk and knowing when to listen are two of the basic skills you need in order to become an excellent conversationalist.

Chapter Eight: Channeling Positivity into Your Conversation to Keep it Going

Before we go any further into this chapter, I want to say congratulations. You have come a long way from where we started and while we still have some ways to go, it is important to sit back and take note of the progress you have made so far. I also hope that at the end of each chapter, you give yourself social assignments to carry out so that you can experiment on the lessons you have learned. This is not the kind of book that you open and read from chapter to chapter, back to back, until the end.

I think that would be boring and at the same time, it will not help you assimilate the information that I have compressed into this book. So, in case you haven't been doing this already, at the end of each chapter (if possible at the end of each segment), close the book and carry out a physical social experiment. Create journals to record your experiences and proffer solutions with a focus on how you think you can improve in those areas you feel you fell short on. Now that we are done with that, let's get right on to the gist of this chapter.

How to Talk and Banter

On the surface level, talk and banter have the same meaning. However, when you go deeper into the definition of things, especially when it comes to conversations, there is a lot of difference. Talk is all we have been doing since we started this journey together from the first chapter. We have been looking at how to talk better, how to engage in small talk and generally just how to be better at talking with people. Banter, on the other hand, is a playful type of conversation. This is the kind of conversation you have with a person whom you are typically attracted to. Sometimes, we have playful conversations with people who are just friends, family members or even people of the same sex. However, for this segment, we are focusing on playful banter with the opposite sex because yes, that is part of communication too.

One major rule of banter conversation is ensuring that both you and the person (s) engaged in the conversation are aware of the fact that everything said in that conversation cannot be taken seriously. You need to apply the law of taking things with the proverbial pinch of salt because everything that you say in that conversation should not be given any kind of levity. The main ingredient for a successful banter conversation is a great sense of humor as well as this mutual understanding that I just talked about. You should be able to roll with the punches and dish out just as much as you are receiving. I have heard of banter conversations that took on a nasty turn and then again, that is not why we are here. We are looking at how to keep the conversation playful and sexy when dealing with the opposite sex without turning ourselves into maniacs.

Another important thing to remember is that banter is a playful exchange and the goal is to tease each other. This is where you display your wit. And as far as I am concerned, there is nothing sexier than wit and humor. In the spirit of keeping things playful and light, your body language should also reflect this. That stern and stiff body posture are not going to work. You need to loosen up a little. That is not to say that you should hunch your back and drop your chin. We talked about this earlier. You have to look confident. But in this case, you also have to look relaxed. Looking stiff and holding your breath at the same time will make you look constipated and I have never known anyone to like that. Finally, you have to learn to have fun with this. You are not writing an exam that your life depends on. You are simply bantering. Also, the only way to become good at bantering is practice. The more you engage in it, the faster you develop the ability to think on your feet.

How to Always have something interesting to Say

Chances are, you have met that one person who is just such a delight to talk to. They always have something to say that stirs up the conversation. That person is what we call a great conversationalist. The thing is, a great conversationalist is not someone who always has something to say. It goes beyond that. After all, is said and done, the best thing about a great conversationalist is the fact that they enter into conversations without any expectations. They don't even try to control the conversation; they just go with the flow. The only time you would find them actively guiding the conversation is when they feel that the topic is veering off into murky waters. Other than that, they just go with it. No matter what is being discussed, they seem to have an idea about it and have the ability to make a valuable contribution to that conversation. This could also be you and here's how to ensure that you always have something interesting to say;

1. Stay up to date on all current events

If you were thinking that the 10 o'clock news was for older people, I am hoping that after this segment, you will change that mindset. The local news basically, is information about what is going on in the world around us. You cannot be so consumed with your life that you fail to be aware of what this is going on. Your awareness of the latest happenings will form a major part of the contribution that you make in any conversation. A great conversationalist always stays updated.

2. Read a book

This book you have in your hand right now will provide a wealth of information that goes beyond just what you were hoping you will get from it when you opened the first page. This is what all books are like. They open you up to a world that you are not familiar with. They transport you to places and times. You can go back in time to visit the past or take a trip to the future. There is just so much information available in a book. Since information is essential for a good conversation, you may need to develop the habit of reading.

3. Think carefully about your answers before you respond

Unlike playful banter, where you allow the first thing that pops into your head to come out of your mouth, this time around you need to think carefully before you respond. At the same time, do not try to force yourself to sound interesting. People can see through your attempts and they would see as someone who is not genuine. In a bid to make yourself sound interesting, you might end up losing the interest of the person you are having a conversation with. Be relaxed, think your answers through and respond in a way that is respectful and befitting of the question you are trying to answer or contribution you are trying to make to that conversation.

How to Resuscitate a Dying Conversation

There are times when no matter how much effort you put into a conversation, we find that things are slowly drifting into a deep end. It is like watching a drunk man trying to walk on a straight line. He has very little control over his limbs and constantly teeters over an imaginary edge. In the same way, you are feeling powerless to stop the death of the conversation. I have been in that situation so many times that I can read the signs of the back of my palm. The banter slowly dies and then people start fidgeting and avoiding each other's gaze. Occasionally, you will hear someone cough here and there. When you see all these signs, know that that conversation is dying. However, it doesn't have to. By injecting your personality into the conversation and taking control of the wheel without necessarily trying to control what people say, you can get the conversation back on track. Here are my tips to help you do so without losing a single drop of sweat

Step one: Don't take it too personally

A lot of times, we assume responsibility for a dying conversation. We feel that it is because we don't have anything to contribute, or we have just too shy to say anything of value that people will find interesting. But this is not the case. Sometimes, people are genuinely tired and when they are tired, a conversation is the last thing on their mind. You have to respect that and don't try to carry the weight of the conversation. If you get the sense that people are tired, let it go. There will always be other times to chat. This is the one time you should accept that it is not your fault. It takes two to dialogue. As long as you tried to put in some effort and you are not getting feedback, you are good.

Step two: Put your newly developed small talk skill to work

If you have been practicing how to engage people with small talk, this is the best time to put it to work. Perhaps the weight of the previous conversation is making people feel uncomfortable. Small talk eases them out of that discomfort and can get the conversation going again. Remember, we talked about the FORD method. This will also be a good place to apply it

Step three: Ask questions and listen attentively to the response

Remember we talked about asking open-ended questions. This is also a great place to put that to work. The questions that we ask will give you more insight into the person and also give them the opportunity to talk (that is if they are interested in talking). I know that previously, I also emphasized the fact that it is the information that you get during this exchange, that will build on the next question. And this is just how you keep going and growing that conversation

Step four: Know when to call it a day

Here's the thing; at some point, you are going to have just to accept that perhaps this person or persons are not interested in having a conversation. And that is okay. It does not reflect directly on your person. We just talked about this in step one; this has to do with the other person. You can't control how they feel about the conversation or their decision to not contribute to the conversation. This is on them and if you are getting this kind of vibe, I would say it is best to check out politely.

How to Come Across as a Positive Person

People naturally gravitate towards someone that they perceive has warm and positive energy. Nobody wants to stand or talk with the bitter crow. And whether you like it or not, there are subconscious vibes that you give off that tells the state of your mind. The subconscious vibe I am talking about here goes beyond your body language. A positive person has a cheery disposition. I would like to point out here that being shy has very little to do with your disposition. I mention this because a lot of people tend to confuse the aversion that shy people have towards social settings with the aversion that a negative person has towards people.

Even if you are shy, it doesn't mean that you are automatically a negative person. A shy person essentially has trouble connecting with people in a social setting and a negative person on the other hand, also experiences trouble connecting people in social settings. But their experiences are not because of the same reasons.

For a negative person, it has more to do with the character traits and dark personality, which makes people avoid them. People don't avoid a shy person, as a matter of fact, because of the quiet nature of the shy person, a lot of people are not even aware of the shy person's presence. But I can tell you that they see a negative person clearly and make a choice to avoid them completely.

To project yourself as a positive person, you would have to do the opposite of everything that the negative person does

1. Do not look down condescendingly on other people

Negative people have a very condescending manner about them. It is almost as if they feel that everyone that they come in contact with is meant to serve them. A positive person, on the other hand, looks at everyone they meet as equals. It doesn't matter your gender, appearance or social status; a positive person automatically finds a way to connect with you. On the other hand, a negative person is looking for reasons to disconnect from you.

2. Do not talk people down when you meet them

This is a classic negative person move. It is all part of the condescending strategy. Sometimes, their talking down on people is not necessarily because they are very mean. They use it to mask their own insecurities. So, if they find that a person is making a more valuable contribution to a conversation than they are, their strategy is to find a way to break that person's confidence. And they do this by talking down on them. A negative person does not appreciate the confidence in a person; instead, they see it as a threat or a challenge. A positive person, on the other hand, is constantly seeking to cheer you on. So, even when people falter in conversations, a positive person does not take that as a limitation or nuisance; instead, they encourage the person.

3. *Do not engage any negative thoughts*

If you are in a social setting, it is possible that the ambiance may not be as beautiful or as up to standard as you would like it to be. And these things could be in your head as you are ruminating on the entire situation. However, a positive person does their best to ensure that what is in their head, stays in their head. As a matter of fact, they go a step further by focusing on the details that are actually nice. That way, the thoughts invoke pleasant feelings and these pleasant feelings radiate into the aura. A negative person, on the other hand, takes delight in tearing apart the efforts of other people. And so they have no trouble thinking negative things and then even going a step further to air out their negative views regardless of who they hurt along the way.

Avoiding Excessive Negativity in Your Social Interactions

Now that you have figured out how to project yourself as a positive person, it is time to look at a scenario where you have other people projecting negativity on you. Just because you are trying to maintain a dialogue and build a relationship doesn't mean that you should have to take on their negativity as well. If you have learned anything along the way, I hope it includes the fact that emotions are contagious. Just as people can contact excitement from your own excitement, you can also catch negative emotions from the negativity of other people. Besides avoiding the concept or the idea of being around negative people, there is also the fact that negativity is an energy-draining exercise. If you have ever been near a with a negative person, you know exactly what I am talking about.

You spend resources, energy and effort trying to fight off that negative spirit and by the time you are done with them, you would feel exhausted. And the worst part is that you wouldn't have made any positive progress. So, resist the urge to be the person who changes the negativity of other people. If you find that you are already feeling emotionally drained every time you encounter a particular person, you need to start looking out for your own mental health. Now, stepping out of that situation takes courage. Especially if you are a shy person who is just learning how to connect with people. If you find out this person you have connected with has such negative energy, it is heartbreaking for starters. Secondly, it is difficult to get out of that situation because you know how much you struggled to even get into the relationship in the first place. But that is what the segment is about.

Before we get into how to avoid negative energy, let us talk about the signs that tell you, you are in a negative environment

1. Someone is getting hurt

In relationships, there will be times where we unintentionally hurt the other person. This kind of hurt is never deliberate and the moment it is brought to the attention of the person who is inflicting that hurt, immediately they feel remorseful and take steps to resolve the situation. However, in a negative environment, the goal is to hurt. Whether you are the one being hurt or you and the person you are with are collaborating to hurt other people, that is a negative situation and you need to get out of it.

2. *You feel as though you are constantly fighting a battle*

Relationships are never easy and that is because you have to diplomatically navigate through your needs, wants and compromises. However, if it feels as though everything in that relationship is an uphill climb, you may want to rethink that situation. Relationships are not really as hard as people say they are. Yes, you will encounter challenges the same when you encounter challenges in life, but if you are constantly fighting and feeling emotionally drained at the end of the day, you need to get out.

3. *You have no sense of self-worth*

Positive relationships have a way of reinforcing your strengths and helping you work on your weaknesses. If you are in a relationship or a situation where you feel that your weaknesses are constantly on display and your confidence is taking a beating on a daily basis, that relationship is very negative. It lacks the nurturing and encouragement that is abundant in positive relationships.

There are many more signs to look out for but these three are classic. So, I urge you to pay attention to. If you find yourself in that situation, it may be hard at first but you need to look out for yourself and take that bold step to get out of that situation. Now, if you are in a networking event or a social setting that has a semblance of a networking event, there is a chance that you would find negative people. Because where you have people in a gathering, you would find clusters of negative energy around the place. You need to step out of those clusters to avoid negative conversations.

This is how to recognize this kind of situation and avoid them:

1. When people are engaging in gossip or hurtful rumors, it may sound delightful to the ears. But remember, someone is getting hurt in that conversation. Even if the person being talked about is not present, you need to get yourself out of that group.

2. When a group of people seems to have nothing positive to say about the event, you can interject and let them know that you see some positive things. If they ignore the things you have highlighted and still go on to talk about their negative perspective, you should take that as your cue to leave that conversation.

3. If you find yourself in a cluster where the body language is dark and unwelcoming, this is a sign that the atmosphere there is negative. You don't even need to wait for a conversation, quietly pick up your things and move to somewhere where the ambiance is more receptive.

Chapter Nine: Using the Art of Storytelling to Drive Conversations

One of my favorite things about my childhood was the bedtime stories that my parents would read to me before I go to bed. More often than not, they prefer to go outside the books that they bought for me because I was the kind of child who got bored with monotony. So, they had to learn how to tell stories that I had never heard before and I tell you, it was the best thing ever. I think that it was because of those bedtime stories that I learned how to be a good storyteller. Even though I was very shy, for the people that I knew and connected with daily, they enjoyed it when I was telling a story.

It could be something as simple as my experience at the office. I learned how to add little embellishments and use certain words to make my story billboard worthy. In this chapter, I am going to draw from my own experiences as well as the opinions of experts to help you perfect the art of telling a good story. This will go on to help you perfect the art of keeping your conversation partners engaged. It is the art of storytelling that makes it possible for a great conversationalist to talk about the weather as though he or she were reading a transcript from one of Sidney Sheldon's novels.

Principles of a Good Storyteller

For starters, a good story is about an event and how the people in that story reacted to that event. A great storyteller has a good story to tell and so for you to become a great storyteller, you have to start with your story. So, let us explore the elements of a good story

1. It comes from an experience

The one thing you should know is that experiences don't have to be something that you went through first-hand. It could be something that you experience through another person. Perhaps it was a story that they shared with you or it was something that you witnessed. Either way, for a story to be good, you need to involve experience. The reason is that when you experience something, you are able to explore that experience with your senses; you know what you felt, or heard or even smelled

2. It should have a series of unexpected events

The twist and turns in the story are what makes it engaging and riveting to the listener. If your story is something that people have heard consistently, over time, they may get bored or not feel half as connected to the story as they would if everything you are laying out with something that was unexpected.

3. It can be embellished but not fabricated

Even the greatest storytellers and fictional writers draw on the experiences of other people to tell their stories. What they write about is not entirely fabricated. There are elements of truth in their stories. What they do however is to embellish the details and make it as unexpected as possible. For an introverted person, this stage here is going to be a very tough hill to climb. However, with some practice, you will get the hang of it.

How to Keep the Other Person Engaged and Listening

In the last segment, our focus was on the elements of a good story. In this segment, we are going to look at how to tell that story. Now, these are two different things but if you are able to bring them together in harmony, you would greatly improve your storytelling skills. So, let us begin

1. Speak in the language that they understand

Storytelling is lost on your listener if they are unable to comprehend you or the things you are saying. Language here goes beyond the commonly accepted native tongue. It is also about vocabulary. If you are talking with children, you would have to bring yourself down to their level and this would also include using words that they can understand. You cannot bring the University standard language into a preschool class and expect that they would understand what you are saying. In the same way, gauge the audience you are with and measure they are receptiveness to your language and then tone it down or up as the case may be, to suit their level of comprehension.

2. Tell your story from a relatable context

If people can't relate to the story that you are telling, there is a very strong possibility that you would lose them. Your message may be a very powerful and life-changing one but if they cannot understand how it impacts them or where they feature in it, you might lose your audience. One way to make your story relatable is to personalize it. Don't approach it with a futuristic perspective or out of body experience. Bring it down to a level where they feel as though they were a part of that story. Emphasize your personal experiences in that story. Highlight what you felt and how you felt and then tie that into the theme of the present conversation you are having.

3. Be animated in the delivery of your story

We talked about voice pitches and voice inflections earlier on and this goes on to emphasize that. When telling a story, if you use the same monotonous tone and expressionless face in your description, you will lose your audience before you get to the end of that story. Try as much as possible to be animated. Let your voice inject as much emotion as possible into the story. Think of it as a stage performance except that you are not on stage and your audience is not paying for your performance. However, the routine is the same. The main actor here is your voice and if you use your voice inflections correctly, you could create different characters in your story and the audience will connect with each of them.

All of this is something that you would have to learn and practice. Some experts recommend taking Improv classes to improve your storytelling skills. I say that is an excellent idea. Go for it if you can.

Chapter Ten: Building Quality Relationships and the Keys to Making Them Last

There is an old African adage that says, "when the handshake extends beyond the elbows, it becomes something else." From the first chapter to the 9th chapter of this book, our focus was establishing the foundation for relationships that first communication you have with people that then goes on to build lasting relationships. Now, we have gone past that proverbial handshake. We are now trying to get to the elbow. This is a different ball game altogether. You would need to learn new skills and this is apart from the ones that you are already developing. Some of it will come naturally to you and some of it will take some patience and understanding to get through it. This chapter is about walking you through that process. I intend to help you build good and healthy relationships no matter how much of an introvert you are.

Connecting with People by Finding Common Ground

Human beings are communal creatures. We are biologically programmed to find and connect with people who we have something in common with. The key to lasting relationships is ensuring that you are connecting with people that you can relate with. If you have nothing in common with this person whatsoever, it can be very difficult for that relationship to thrive. And the reason for this is because at some point it would seem as though the relationship is one-sided. When a relationship becomes one-sided, it becomes a breeding ground for resentment.

Today, the world has experienced the highest rate of divorce than it ever has in recent years. And if you look closely at the people involved and have a conversation with them, you would find that the whole relationship crumbled because of resentment. I have listened to interviews of people who were getting divorced or trying to salvage a damaged relationship, one of the recurrent themes in those conversations was the fact that they felt like they no longer had anything in common with this person. It is very important to have common grounds in a relationship and so before you even get into it, you have to ensure that both parties have something in common.

It could be a business goal if you are talking about formal relationships. Or shared values and belief systems if you are talking about informal relationships. Do not connect with people based on trivial things like their appearance or wealth. Over time, those things will fade away. The important things to look for are their character traits, their personalities, their dreams, and their ambitions. These are things that remain consistent over time. And when you get to know these things, you have to be able to see where you fit in because your fitting into their world as well as their fitting into your world establishes common ground. That way both worlds can come together without colliding. Lasting relationships are built through the merging of worlds and it starts from finding common ground.

How to Make Them Feel You Empathize

In today's world, the concept of empathy has evolved from its original meaning. Without going through the whole psychological babble, let me just put it this way; empathy is basically walking in the other person's shoes. In other words, you put yourself in that person's situation and have a second-hand experience of what they are going through. Today, a lot of people feel that empathy is about saying nice things when people are going through stuff. That is not empathy. That is being kind and showing compassion. Empathy allows you to understand a person's point of view and like I said, for you to be able to do that, you would have to walk in their shoes. In this case, it doesn't have to mean you going through exactly what they are going through. You would have to put your imagination to work. Picture the circumstances that they are going through, insert yourself in that situation and then look at things from that perspective. This will give you a unique understanding of a person's behavior, thoughts, and motives.

In relationships, we tend to focus on our needs and this is because we fail to empathize with those of our partners. When someone reacts to you or something that you did, we take it personally because we feel that it is more about us than them. While I am a strong advocate for making yourself the number one lead character in your life, I feel that if you want your relationship to thrive, you may have to get off your soapbox from time to time and view things from the other person's perspective. When you have the perspective of the other person, you are able to contribute in a more valuable way to that relationship. For example, a couple where one spouse stays at home and the other goes to work every day would have to struggle with resentment if either of the spouses does not take the time to recognize the contributions of the other. And to recognize these contributions of the other person, one person would need to picture themselves in the shoes.

If the partner that does not see how difficult it is to manage the children at home and then keep the home in order, they would fail to appreciate the homeliness that they always come to meet at the end of their workday. And this is because they are more focused on the tedious activities they had to face in the office. This also goes vice versa. For couples in the same situation who empathize with each other, you would find them carrying out activities to make the life of their partners easier. The one who comes home from work would not immediately start requesting things; instead they look for areas where they can contribute to the upkeep of the home. And the same goes for the person who was at home. They would not make demands as soon as the other person comes home. Instead, they will give them space to allow them mentally decompress. This is what it means to empathize with people.

How Listening Can Help You See and Make Connections

When you have an emotional need or concern, you are most likely going to go to a person who you feel would listen to you. This also works with people in a relationship. They tend to air their views to people they feel will sympathize and listen to them. This often comes into play when we are thinking of the male and female dynamics in relationships. Men are not really talkers or great communicators are generally speaking in one on one relationships. They are actionable in nature and tend to be more of doers. Women, on the other hand, invest a lot in communicating their emotions and feelings.

The problem arises when the man feels that every time the woman says something, he has to do something about what she has said. But in reality, more often than not, what the woman needs is someone who would listen to what she is saying and sympathize with her. Listening, in this case, is not just about keeping your mouth shut and leaving your ears open. It goes beyond that. Earlier on, when I was talking about the art of small talk, I did say that one of the things you need to learn is how to actively listen and listening in this context also applies the same way.

You have to pay attention to what the person is saying so that you can hear them and then understand where they are coming from. It also helps you to empathize with the person. If you are able to actively listen to the people you are in a relationship with, you will find that you automatically become their confident. More than that, because you paid attention to what they are saying and you are able to understand and empathize with them, you are put in a better position to proffer solutions to their problems.

Everybody loves to be in a relationship with a problem solver and so it is important that you pay attention to what is being said. In the same vein, do not enter into every conversation with the intention to fix the other person because then every time they have a conversation with you, you would find it difficult to hear them out. This is most likely because you are already playing these scenarios in your head where you are fixing things.

You are not the human equivalent of correction fluid. It is ok if you don't fix a situation. Sometimes, all you need to do is just listen. Everything starts with active listening.

How to make them feel like your family

Family is one of those relationships in life that we have absolutely no control over. You do not choose who your biological relations are. You are basically born into them. However, when you start socializing, you are making a conscious decision to choose who you relate with and sometimes those relations that you build create a bond that can be likened to that of a family. The love, respect and loyalty in that relationship are enough to cement your bond for a long time. But how the people get from the point of being strangers to that place where they feel like this person they are with is a relationship for a lifetime? The main ingredients there is you. As I said earlier, when it comes to families, you have no choice in that matter. But in this situation, you are in complete control.

Without realizing it, we have been given the power to decide how long our relationships last. And before you try to make that argument, yes, it takes two or more to build a relationship. But it also comes from a conscious decision on your part. You would still need to be the one to apply certain principles and boundaries to enable that relationship to thrive. When you put a plant in soil, it is biologically programmed to grow. However, there are things you can do to ensure that the plant experiences excellent growth so that it is able to flourish and bear fruit. This phenomenon also applies to relationships. As humans, we are biologically programmed to connect with each other, but it requires effort on your part to foster and nurture that connection into a long-lasting relationship. When someone becomes your family, you are saying to that person that they are more than their flaws and mistakes. And that they have earned your loyalty and your trust and regardless of what happens in the future, you would always be there for them. There is also the unspoken expectation that they would also accept you in the same way.

I would like to insert here that it is important to ensure that the feeling is mutual. If not, you are setting yourself up for disappointment. Expectations have killed a lot of relationships mostly because we expect things that we can't give or we give things that we don't expect from the other person. There has to be a balance. If the relationship has that mutual feeling, the progression from the level of strangers to the family will take a natural turn. In fact, you probably would not even need to utter those words out loud. It is an unspoken commitment. My advice is this, you have been given an opportunity now to choose who you call family, apply due diligence in that process and most importantly, obey the golden rule of relationships; treat people as you expect to be treated.

The Difference Between Sincere and Fake

Let me start this segment by stating it categorically that if you are faking anything in a relationship, you have laid a foundation for dishonesty. A healthy relationship thrives on sincerity and openness. If there are areas where you have to fake communication and genuine affection for that person, I hate to be the one to break the news to you, but that is not a healthy relationship. If you have ever been at the receiving end of fake sincerity, you would understand how hurtful it is. There are people who manipulate their way into relationships to achieve a certain gain. For them, it is all about their goals and not about the needs of the person that they are in a relationship with. If this is you, I would advise you to desist from that. However, to prevent a situation where you are at the other end, here is how you can spot a fake from the real.

1. It feels too good to be true

Everybody wants to live in a fairytale and a lot of times, because of this idea that we have in our heads, we ignore signs that are glaring at us and focus on those things that we want in that relationship. So, instead of seeing the warning labels, we put on our rose-tinted glasses and ride on the highs that this relationship gives to us. If you find that everything appears to be perfect in your relationship, there is something missing. As I said earlier, relationships are not as complicated as we make it out to be; however, there are bound to be challenged. If yours is free from challenges and it is looking like it is straight out of a fairy tale novel, take a long pause and reevaluate that relationship.

2. You have a sense that something is wrong

Our instincts are designed to alert us to dangers or threats in our environment. In a relationship, if you get the sense that something is wrong, even though you just can't place your finger on it, there is a very strong possibility that something is actually wrong. You can either decide to become a Nancy Drew in that relationship and do some behind the scenes detective work or step back until you are able to figure things out. Either way, something is off and that is your instinct telling you that perhaps your relationship is lacking sincerity you desire.

3. *Nobody around you seems to like this person*

Now, this is a big red flag. No matter how unlikable a person may be, to an extent, you would still find people who would be rooting for them. However, if you find that the people with whom you share a close relationship within your life are unable to accept this new person, there is a chance that they see something that you cannot. And a lot of times, that thing that they are seeing is the insincerity of this person's actions.

Timing a Sincere Compliment and How to Insert it into the Flow of the Conversation

Complimenting someone in the conversation is a way of affirming your appreciation of the person with whom you are conversing with. However, you have to ensure that the compliment you are giving is appropriate to the circumstance. In a formal setting, for instance, you cannot make compliments about a person's body part. Even if they are about things that are innocent like their Eyes or nose. It would make the person feel uncomfortable and an awkward silence could ensue. Your component should be about a personality trait or their contribution to their profession.

Outside that, the next thing you need to focus on is how you deliver the compliment. You want the high praise that you are offering to the person to come off as natural as possible without seeming as though you have an ulterior motive. In my experience, I believe that the best way to achieve that is to avoid lingering on the compliment for too long, especially if you are in a crowded space. If you have a one on one conversation with the person, of course, you could go on to emphasize that particular compliment. However, you should also note that if that one on one conversation is being carried out in a formal setting, it is best to avoid lingering on that compliment. Simply say what you want to say in the most sincere way devoid of offensive words and then move on.

The art of the compliment (without sucking up to the other person)

For this part, I would say your intentions matter a lot. If you intend to suck up to a person, the compliments that you offer to them will actually come off as that sucking up. Because it would lack the genuineness that is required when offering compliments. Again, you should also avoid lingering on the compliments that you give or constantly repeating them. This is only appropriate when you are in a very close, informal relationship with a person. Perhaps, your friend or your romantic partner. In that scenario, I think you need to linger on your compliments as often and as long as you can.

Another mistake that people make when it comes to paying compliments to people is that they feel if you compliment a person, you cannot find something wrong with them. That is not true. It is possible that you like a person's display of empathy; however, you may have a problem with how intense they are in those moments. And because you care about this person, you call them out on it. In healthy relationships, whether formal or informal, genuine compliments go hand-in-hand with constructive criticisms. If you find that you are unable to criticize a person even though you see glaring things that they are doing wrong, but you constantly find yourself complimenting them, it is safe to say that you are sucking up to them.

Chapter Eleven: Social Interactions in a Group Setting

Now, we have come to the moment of truth. In the previous chapters, we looked at initiating conversations with people one on one as well as inserting yourself into groups. Now, we are going to take things a step further. We are no longer looking at establishing a relationship with one person. We are looking at how you can carry a group along. And in this context, I am not just going to focus on networking in groups. I would look at you being a public speaker. I know that for an introvert, this is a giant leap, but that is how much faith I have in you. Because if I was able to go from being this shy kid to this person who is always excited to get on stage, I believe that so can you.

Group Conversation Flow

In a group conversation, three things can happen. You are either under the spotlight, which means you are the main person championing the conversation. Or you could be a spectator, which means that you are the one who listens more than you speak. Then you have the last situation, which I feel is the most ideal situation; you are sharing the spotlight with all the people in the group. To ensure that you are not lost in that group conversation, the first thing you need to do is identify what role you are playing.

Are you going to be in the spotlight? If you are under the spotlight, it means that you have to be the one leading the conversation, and by leading the conversation, it does not necessarily mean that you are the only one talking. Remember what I said about great conversationalists. They don't take control of the conversation. Somehow, they are able to immerse themselves in the conversation and still give everyone the room to express themselves. If you would rather play the role of the listener, you need to be an active listener. And that means you pay attention to what is being said. Understand what the person is saying and where they are coming from and then interject occasionally with questions based on the information you have received. Try as much as possible not to go off point

And finally, if you are in the last scenario where everyone is sharing the spotlight, the key to balancing it is to be both the listener and the person under the spotlight. You listen to people talking, get their point of view and then assert yourself in the conversation. There are people who have a tendency to want to talk you down. It is your responsibility to take control of your own voice. Not by increasing the pitch of your voice but by ensuring that you assert yourself. That way, you are making yourself heard and are actively contributing to the flow of the conversation.

How to Join an Existing Group Conversation

Unless you are aiming for drama, I will suggest that you enter the group as quietly as possible. And then before you make a speech, listen to what is being said. Hear the views and opinions of the people that are talking in that group and then based on the information that you get; you can then ask a question. Be warned, though; do not go into the conversation with your guns blazing. That spreads hostility and may make the people in that group feel a little bit resentful of you. Even though your point may be just what they need to get the conversation going, you need to take the gentle approach.

As you continue contributing to that conversation, you can take off your gloves and then get into it really deep. The reason I asked that you delay a little before asserting yourself is so that you are able to get your bearings. Understand what the conversation is about, know where most of the people in that group stand regarding the conversation and then assert yourself to make your own contribution. When you listen, you are able to understand more and when you understand more, you are less likely going to make a fool of yourself. This is after all our biggest fears when we get into conversations that involve groups of people.

Group Conversation Guidelines and Principles for Standing Out and Making a Connection

This here is where you learn the art of public speaking. I understand that right now you are not a public speaker, and you probably have no intention of becoming one. But at some point in your life, you may be called upon to address a group of at least ten people. If you start practicing and preparing yourself for that moment, when that time comes, you will find that you are able to have a conversation with your crowd easily and you would do this without fretting or panicking.

The key thing there is to apply everything you have learned so far. But instead of focusing on just one person, focus on the group in the room. The technique I usually use is to have the mindset that I am talking to one person but act as though I am communicating with the group. So, I try as much as possible to use the space that is available to me. For instance, if you are standing on an elevated podium, staying still in one spot does not really help you engage your crowd. You need to take a few steps at a time and keep your eyes on the crowd. You can choose a certain spot to concentrate your gaze on. Occasionally and from time-to-time, let your gaze go over the people in the other parts of the room.

Be as animated as possible in your conversation. Let your hand gestures be appropriate but do not standstill. And finally, put everything you have learned on the art of storytelling to good use. Be clear in whatever message you are trying to pass across. Let it have its starting point in a story and the story should be something that your audience can relate with. Also remember, language is important. Speak in a language that the crowd will understand and avoid the use of offensive words. For this last part, pretend as though your very existence is dependent on it. Because offending one person in a one on one conversation is bad enough. To do it in a group, that could spell the end of your career and affect your ability to speak in public.

And with that, we have come to the end of this book. But don't close it yet, I still have a few words to share with you.

Conclusion

Once again, I am so proud of how far you have come on this journey, and I am deeply honored that I was involved (even if it was in the tiniest way) to help you overcome your social anxiety and become a better version of yourself. Relationships are important. No matter the lies we tell ourselves because of our hurts and past experiences, we still need people around us. With this in mind, I would like you to subscribe to the knowledge that you are in control of the relationships that you develop in your life. You may not be able to control the actions that people take. However, you have a strong voice in determining the kind of people who stay in your life and those who don't.

Going forward, I want you to develop this mindset as you deal with people. Not everybody has to be your best friend and not everybody has to like you. You are important as a person and you deserve to be treated as though you are important. So, choose people who choose you. Treat people the way you want to be treated. You do not deserve anything less. We may have come to the end of this book but believe me when I say that your journey is just beginning. And if you can step outside of your comfort zone, I can guarantee you that life outside your door is going to be exciting and fun. There is nothing to be scared of.

Even when people tell you 'no,' that word carries a blessing. That 'no' is basically sparing you from the heartache of what the relationship would have been if they said 'yes.' And so, rejection is not the ultimate definition of your life. Some of the people you encounter would choose to walk away from you. That is ok, in my opinion, perfect even. Your mantra going forward should be "***choose people who choose me***." I wish you all the best in your professional and social life. And I hope that from this book, you are able to become better at communication and for that reason, you are able to build better relationships. Please remember to pay it forward by passing the knowledge you have gained here to other people in your shoes.

From me and everyone who contributed to making this book a success, we are sending love, light and laughter to you.

References

Common Strategies: Common Persuasion Techniques. (n.d.). Retrieved from https://www.psychologistworld.com/behavior/compliance/strategies/overview

Eisenhauer, T. .(n.d). How to Use the Persuasion Principle of "Authority" at Work. Retrieved from https://axerosolutions.com/blogs/timeisenhauer/pulse/837/how-to-use-the-persuasion-principle-of-authority-at-work

Green, J. (2017). How to Prime Prospects to Sat "Yes" (and Make the Sale). Retrieved from https://www.phoneburner.com/blog/how-to-prime-prospects-to-say-yes/

Harmer, S. (n.d). 8 Ways To Stop Emotional Manipulation. Retrieved from https://www.lifehack.org/articles/lifestyle/8-ways-stop-emotional-manipulation.html

Layton, J. (n.d). How Brainwashing Works. Retrieved from https://science.howstuffworks.com/life/inside-the-mind/human-brain/brainwashing.htm

Making a Great First Impression. (n.d). Retrieved from https://www.mindtools.com/CommSkll/FirstImpressions.htm

Mobley, C. (2014). Softening the Sharps and tuning up normal. Retrieved from https://purposefulfaith.com/harsh-words/

Nicholson, J. (2018). 4 Ways to Use Scarcity to Persuade and Influence. Retrieved from https://www.psychologytoday.com/us/blog/persuasion-bias-and-choice/201812/4-ways-use-scarcity-persuade-and-influence

Reciprocity technique #1: pre-giving. (n.d). Retrieved from https://gohighbrow.com/reciprocity-technique-1-pre-giving/

Stillman, J. (n.d). 10 Techniques Used by Manipulators (and How to Fight Them). Retrieved from https://www.inc.com/jessica-stillman/10-popular-techniques-used-by-manipulators-and-how-to-fight-them.html

The Zeigarnik Effect Explained. (n.d). Retrieved from https://www.psychologistworld.com/memory/zeigarnik-effect-interruptions-memory

Tyrrell, M. (2014). Master Hypnotic Language Patterns in 3 Straightforward Steps. Retrieved from https://www.unk.com/blog/3-steps-to-hypnotic-language-mastery/

be your own psychic – 5 steps to give yourself a psychic reading. (n.d). Retrieved from https://www.micheleknight.com/articles/psychic/psychic-ability/be-your-own-psychic-5-steps-to-give-yourself-a-psychic-reading/

Cherry, K. (2019). Understanding Body Language and Facial Expressions. Retrieved from https://www.verywellmind.com/understand-body-language-and-facial-expressions-4147228

Chu, M. (2017). The Truth About How Gut Instincts Really Work. Retrieved from https://medium.com/the-mission/the-truth-about-how-gut-instincts-really-work-d665425f1eb1

English, J. (2019). 5 Basic Body Language Signals of Manipulators. Retrieved from https://drwebercoaching.com/5-basic-body-language-signals-of-manipulators/

How To Read People Like the FBI. (2018). Retrieved from https://www.thrivetalk.com/how-to-read-people/

Kloppers. M (n.d). Dealing with Liars. Retrieved from https://www.mentalhelp.net/blogs/dealing-with-liars/

Orloff, J. (2014). The Power of Surrender: Let Go and Energize Your Relationships, Success, and Well-Being [pdf]. Retrieved from https://www.amazon.com/Power-Surrender-Energize-Relationships-Well-Being/dp/0307338215/ref=as_li_ss_tl?ie=UTF8&redirect=true&linkCode=sl1&tag=theminwor01-20&linkId=7bec015a8cfbec80e5bb69f63a7ca784

Scott, R. (n.d). How to Read Body Language – Revealing the Secrets Behind Common Nonverbal Cues. Retrieved from https://fremont.edu/how-to-read-body-language-revealing-the-secrets-behind-common-nonverbal-cues/

Selig, M. (2016). Know Yourself? 6 Specific Ways to Know Who You Are. Retrieved from https://www.psychologytoday.com/us/blog/changepower/201603/know-yourself-6-specific-ways-know-who-you-are

9 Personality Types – Enneagram Numbers. (n.d). Retrieved from https://www.theworldcounts.com/life/potentials/9-personality-types-enneagram-numbers

About the Author

Jason Miller is a bestselling author and human psychology researcher, a dedicated student of the human condition. Obsessed with self-improvement and fascinated by the power of the mind, his personal mission is to help people realize their full potential and reach higher levels of fulfillment and consciousness.

Jason writes books that focus on changing old habits, overcoming self-destructing behavior and the best strategies on how to deal with rejection. He is based in Los Angeles, California. Jason possesses a BSc in psychology and a graduate degree and has worked with many people from all walks of life.

www.ingramcontent.com/pod-product-compliance
Ingram Content Group UK Ltd.
Pitfield, Milton Keynes, MK11 3LW, UK
UKHW060645281025
8632UKWH00004B/43